Conquered Fool

Lake Publishing
P.O. Box 1
Hardy, VA 24101
United States of America

Library of Congress Control Number: 2022901974

ISBN: 979-8-9854987-0-7   (hardcover)
ISBN: 979-8-9854987-1-4   (paperback)
ISBN: 979-8-9854987-2-1   (e-book)

BISAC Codes
1. PHI000000   PHILOSOPHY / Natural
2. REL006080   RELIGION / Biblical Criticism & Interpretation
3. SOC072000   SOCIAL SCIENCE / Activism & Social Justice

Conquered Fool by David Allan
First Edition - 2022

Dedicated to Jan, Mike, Mom and Dad, and countless others.

Contents of Conquered Fool

Introduction to Conquered Fool

This anthology is selected writings from throughout the years. In general, the work is arranged in chronological order by the date written, oldest to newest. It is comprised of the two *Selfish Young Man* books, plus a variety of articles, commentaries and poems, written later and grouped together as *Wiser Old Man*.

There are also two letters in the last book as I see potential benefit for some readers by sharing them. The first was in response to a dear friend who was rattled by my first book and sent me a letter that was entirely Bible verses. The second was a thank you note to a business client with whom I shared some of my personal beliefs.

In addition, I answered a number of questions put to me prior to publishing this anthology.

Everything herein is non-fiction, or at least as I believe things to be, with the exception of the separate poetry section in *Wiser Old Man*. Most of those poems were written for entertainment or encouragement, and therefore a few of them have some embellishments. I considered omitting them, but realized their inclusion should not diminish the integrity of my serious writing for level-headed thinkers. The fact is, life would be so out of balance without humor and imagination that it wouldn't be worth living. Hateful people aren't likely to consider my opinions anyway. If they want to focus on finding faults, so be it. I'm far from perfect. Let's move on...

Selfish Young Man

Contents of Selfish Young Man

Introduction

An Honest Look At

- Scriptures
- Denominations
- The Pharisees
- Wolves in Sheep's Clothing
- Women Ministers
- Holy Days
- We Are Gods
- Marriage in Heaven
- Eternal Hell
- The Trinity
- A God Grows Up
- The Law Fails
- Mistakes
- Judas
- Satan
- Prophecy
- Playing God
- Time Does Not Exist
- Different Realities
- The Bride of Christ
- Equality and the Sexes
- Inexorable Conclusions

Contents of Selfish Young Man (continued)

Commentaries and Encouragement

Personal

Notes

Introduction to Selfish Young Man

So many good things have been given to me during my life, so many hand outs and hand ups. But youth, and the selfish ingratitude that goes with it, blinded me from realizing how deeply indebted I am to those who went before me. This book is a small effort at repayment, given to those who still struggle like me, and those who will follow.

It is not possible that all of my viewpoints will make sense to you, nor should they, for we are all individuals and therefore different by definition. But we are all human, so I know having written open and honestly that some of my perspectives may be of value to you.

I will say this very plainly at the onset: Jesus would be grieved to hear some of the words that have been put in his mouth and to see what some organizations have turned his legacy into.

Although some individual churches may be of benefit to the spiritually dead or spiritually young, organized religions are useless. Generally speaking, the origins of all religions are based on sparks of enlightenment that have been warped into businesses and seats of power by egotistical people. False doctrines abound, presented like facts by charlatans who dare tell us they speak for God, as if they have some access to the Almighty that the rest of us do not.

The Christian religions, like all other religions, are a waste of time for spiritual adults. True religion is a personal matter and nothing about it, except love, is universal to us all.

The bottom line is that we are all gods, we are all christs, we are all members of the spirit, and Love is the only real authority that ever has, does, or will exist.

What I try to do in this book is to address some of these false religious doctrines, making corrections and explaining a number of other little understood things that both the scriptures and common sense reasoning reveal. In addition, I include a variety of essays on other topics and also share some of my personal experiences. My most important objective is to bridge the gap between religion and love, which should be the same thing, but are not in most churches. My hope is to help people realize the childishness of following someone else's opinion about the meaning and mysteries of life, which is what organized religions are, encouraging people instead to regard the spirit of love within them as the only real authority.

Although we should try to listen carefully to each other's opinions, as we will almost always learn something, we should never subordinate the honest opinions of our heart to someone else's. Therefore, if you and I are both subject to the authority of love, while I may decide your opinion is not right for me, perhaps utterly reject it, not only will I tolerate your view point, I will defend your right to it.

I do not claim all the answers and opinions I put forth here are certain, except as they pertain to me, at this point in time. Indeed, it concerns me that time may reveal to me that some of my understanding was weak, perhaps even wrong. Often I reach a conclusion, only to learn something new that sheds better light and presents more questions. In the past, my reaction to that was to rewrite the part in question to reflect the better understanding. However, it is not possible to understand everything. And if a person waited to speak until he did know everything, then that person would never speak at all. But you can understand to the point of satisfaction, and this point is where I am. So when you judge my effort, I ask you consider: Did I at least get you to think and shed a little light somewhere? Read it, get out of it what you can, leave the rest behind.

I used a number of quotes from the Christian scriptures (sometimes as I recalled them, so they may be paraphrased). Some of the references and their subsequent logical conclusions will not be understood by readers who have not extensively studied the Bible. But everything one really needs to know can be seen through natural philosophy anyway, so even the layman should understand much of what I have to say. I also noted some of the scriptures I referred to so people could more easily find passages they may not be familiar with.

If you are not familiar with the scriptures of various religions, you might consider reading them. I think anyone who has, with an open mind, has benefited a little. However, understand that none of them are truly important and their endless study becomes a waste of time. This is because the spirit of "love one another" is a part of us all, as it always has been, so we all have access to this vastly superior information, if only we will listen.

Criticism of the things I have expressed in this book is certain. So be it. My only response is to say that I have examined myself closely and my heart is right with the spirit, at least as it concerns what I have written. It was the best I could do and I held nothing back if I thought it might help, even to my own embarrassment.

Again, I owe so many people who have done right by me over the years, many of whom did not get back anything of the sort. I sincerely thank you all.

David Allan

An Honest Look At

Scriptures

The origin of the writings that became the Christian scriptures is something that most churches never share with their flocks. The following is a very brief overview of the history of those documents, the entirety of which is presented in very general terms.

The first gentile Christian churches had no writings whatsoever for about the first 40 years after Jesus' death. Everything was oral, with people assembling at individual homes and taking turns speaking about whatever they believed was inspired or edifying. Most of these people were converts from pagan religions in which they were already actively involved. Stories about Jesus and anything that might be related to his teaching were the main focus in these assemblies. Individual speaking being what it is, the tales passed from person to person and town to town with omissions or embellishments, pieces remembered incorrectly, or with things misunderstood, sometimes including various fabrications for whatever reason. In short, the stories were never retold exactly the same way in any two places.

Some of these stories eventually found their way into written form, whether mostly or partially true, or not at all. Within a few more decades there were also various letters from Christian leaders. Many of these assorted writings were copied and passed along over time, though not always written the same way when reproduced, and virtually never the same when translated. Given the nature and wisdom of man, even the original orations, written stories, and letters would have contained personal bias, errors, and omissions.

Within 100 years of Christ's death, most individual churches were collecting, some even creating various writings, which were administered by the budding hierarchy of administrators in those churches. The original writings that sprang up in these first churches were sometimes copied and shared with other churches, who then might share their copies with still more churches, and so on and so forth. This resulted in versions of the original writings that varied from one church to another, the differences ranging from just a little to very different. Where these scrolls or codices had gaps or obvious errors, church administrators might fill them in with whatever they deemed most advantageous for their self-interests, though usually they used their best opinions, although not always right.

The churches in some larger cities and a few small towns had outgrown meeting at just one home, so they coordinated meetings in public places, wherever they were not persecuted. They used multiple homes or clandestine get-togethers in the bigger cities where they were unwelcome.

In these churches, increasingly springing up throughout the Roman Empire, there was also a movement away from the original church structure. What was once a group of equals was vanishing. Meetings wherein any member of the church could take a turn speaking as a teacher, sharing whatever moved them, were rapidly fading away. By the time 200 years had passed after Jesus' death, the original emphasis in most churches had nearly completely changed. Now only a select few administrators and leaders would regularly speak at their meetings. Often they would read from the plethora of writings they had by now accumulated and kept at that particular church, then give their opinions and comments while the majority of people quietly listened. In just a few generations the message of the christ Jesus had been altered dramatically, as were the original writings about his teachings to match the changing emphases. This is all the greater loss given the original documents were imperfect in the first place.

By the time organized religion had taken full control of Jesus' legacy, some 300 years after his death, Christianity was very public in some places and as widespread as the paganism that preceded it.

Administrative hierarchy existed in virtually every local church, and these people officiated virtually every aspect of every meeting. In their preaching they utilized a wide variety of the various versions of the many handwritten letters and stories that we now call "books" of the Bible. Also, by this time, nearly every gentile church had added enormous portions of the Old Testament writings from the Jews, which tripled the amount of words from which to draw material to craft sermons. Christianity was, in fact, becoming a very big business throughout the Roman Empire, steadily replacing the religious business of paganism and its unique mythologies.

Every individual church (there were no religions) used a different Bible, meaning a different collection of these "books." And in small to very large amounts, each of these books varied from the story or letter by the same name that might be in the Bible of another town's church.

Over time, as these churches evolved into political powers and businesses, administrators were able to push towards some standardization of their texts. In other words, since differences between churches injured their credibility, meetings started happening among neighboring church leaders, who then tried to decide which books, and which versions, would be best for them to use. Surely there were people who had good intentions by such things. But when we see how the early church, as a whole, moved away from the equality that humble Jesus preached, and turned itself into businesses and positions of power, this is all the proof we need to reject these organizations.

We must also, in general, reject most of the scriptures as inspired by God. Common sense is more than enough to show it too, if we just allow ourselves to think. The nature of mankind being what it is, coupled with documented history, shows that each passing generation of early church administrators tinkered with the original writings they assembled for their own self-interests. Within a few hundred years after the death of Jesus, almost the entirety of Jesus' original message was lost or altered. All but gone was the story of a demon who found the key to life (love one another) and tried to help us other demons find their way.

The historical record indicates these early churches and their leaders had thousands upon thousands of heated doctrinal arguments with each other, which means that the people of their congregations had millions of disagreements over how to interpret what was meant by this, or what was meant by that.

However, the businessmen who took control of Jesus' legacy were able to agree on one thing: If they put Jesus above us, then they could be above us in his absence.

Abuses by the then established Christian churches continued to grow after this period almost totally unchecked, for about 1000 years, until about 700 years ago. The seeds of reform were slowly developing by then, and it was at this time that a few scattered individuals set about to

15

divide the books of the Bible into chapters. The success of their various works gave encouragement to the next step, about 200 years later, when other individuals set about to number all the passages, sentences, and verses.

Once divided and numbered, most subsequent translators and scribes have been afraid to correct any errors that resulted from parceling documents that were reproductions of inferior manuscripts, which were never perfect in the first place. Understand, the first numbered versions were copies of copies, of copies of copies of copies... easily the 100th version of the original in many cases. After the chapter divisions and subsequent numberings, corrections of some of the mistakes and fictional additions became impossible in the minds of most translators and scribes that followed. Therefore, they simply smoothed over any gaps or inaccuracies that resulted from omissions, additions, and rearrangements as best as they could.

In short, after centuries of tampering with the ever decreasing original writings that became scriptures, it finally became difficult to keep altering them. On the other hand, all the lies and mistakes made earlier were virtually cemented in place.

It was also around this time that the printing press was invented. This effectively gave the particular versions that were mass produced a more official status, deservedly or not.

In conclusion, the Christian scriptures are a mess, and they have been from the very beginning. But the facts about the origin of these books we call the Bible are seldom told by clergy to the laity.

Some ministers are so uninformed or compromised that they even say the Bible is the unquestionable Word of God.

Denominations

Which denomination is best? None of them. It can be surprising what some ministers and religious people will say in their arrogance, but pride is pride – and party spirit is just another form of it.

If an individual begins thinking that he is better than other people, then that person goes astray and the spirit is displeased. So how does being a group of individuals improve the same mistake?

The only intelligent way to judge a church is on an individual basis. By definition, a church is comprised of people, so the quality of a particular church is almost completely dependent on its ministers and congregation. Churches should not be franchised like businesses, and Christianity (and all religions) would be better off with no denominations at all, rather letting every individual church stand or fall on its own merits.

If a church develops branches, that is very good, but they must be independent after they mature. This is just the same as how children are managed by their parents until maturity, but then afterwards report directly to the spirit within them, meaning their own consciences.

After all, finding one's salvation happens the same way it has in every day and age – we accept the authority of love. It is never by being a member of a particular group. If being a Jew is not sufficient to save those that are found to be false, even though Jesus himself was a Jew, then how can being a member of a particular brand of Christianity save us?

The Apostle Paul saw the very beginning of this sort of partisanship and rebuked those churches sharply, for some were claiming Paul as their leader, others Apollos, and yet others Peter.[1] But Paul put a stop to their rivalry by explaining that Jesus was their real leader. And I would add that Jesus pointed towards the spirit of God as the real guide, and that the spirit shows us that love is the only real authority people must follow.

The Pharisees

There is a popular misconception among many churchgoers that most people who do not attend church are lost souls, while most that do attend have found salvation.

That idea is very wrong since many of the elect (people who have decided to be obedient to the authority of love) never attend church, and among the people that do, many of them are not at all ruled by love.

The people who do attend church seem to fall into several distinct categories.

The first and oftentimes smallest group is the real believers. Formerly unwilling to accept the authority of love, they were won over by the word of their lord and the spirit at large. Having truly repented from the heart, their new and changing behaviors are positive proof of new persons in progress.

The second group is comprised of those that are as yet unwilling to accept the authority of love, but are making an effort to hear what the way is all about. From here they will decide to believe it, reject it, or pretend to believe it; and this group, the pretenders, is the third main group in most of today's churches.

I call this last group the "Pharisees" in sarcastic honor of their predecessors, and today's equivalent is no less a challenge since all their efforts are either to magnify themselves, or to conceal their disobedience to loving each other

Just as yesterday's Pharisees were filled with pride to be associated with the temple, so it is that their modern counterparts love the word "Christian" and to be associated with the church. But the reason is only to flatter themselves or to obtain recognition from others. Indeed, they often use their association with a church like a stick to prod others into flattering them with how righteous they are, but whenever they witness to anyone the only thing they really say is "I am better than you."

But all of this is no surprise, since the impact of this type of person has always been a burden on those who genuinely seek to understand spiritual things.

In Moses' day, though all the people were set free from physical slavery, only a few of their number found favor.

Were things any better in Jesus' day? Not much, for though all the people had the opportunity to be set free from spiritual slavery, having heard Jesus' message to love one another, only a few really changed their selfish ways. But the wise understand that now is always the time to submit to the authority of love, instead of experiencing the second death later. Therefore, they reject their selfish pride and admit their past foolishness before the spirit.

As for the trials some say submitting to Jesus' message brings, that is just not true. Such trials are only illusions. Love carries its own happiness, for once it is embraced it takes root, and this creates a metamorphosis in our souls, a light in the dark.

So when today's pharisees cause trouble, remember that the people of today are not much different than the people who went before us.

Wolves in Sheep's Clothing

Even worse than the many false believers in today's churches are the people who sometimes lead them. The Apostles spoke about these ministers of Satan and forewarned us of their arrival, noting that some had already managed to creep into positions of leadership. How much more so now then, with all these years gone by?

Outwardly friendly and caring, but inside arrogant and crafty, some ministers cleverly maneuver to amass great material wealth. Others are fiercely proud of their imaginary stature, always ready to quietly tear anyone to pieces who would dare question them. But Jesus said we could recognize them by their "fruits," and indeed we do, for their deeds speak loud and clear.

Some ministers actually demand we tithe 10% of our income to them, telling us how the Old Testament commands it. Then they turn around and correctly explain that the old law is dead and buried by the risen christ Jesus. Shameful contradiction.

There are other popular approaches for bringing in lots of money. One is to deliver sermons that humiliate anyone unwilling to give generously. Another is to imply that our donations bring us closer to salvation. The first example is cruelty for the sake of money, but the second is even worse. Utterly wicked and very dangerous religion, it implies salvation can be purchased.

The Apostle Paul warns: "I may have such absolute faith that I can move hills from their place, but if I have no love, I count for nothing: I may distribute all I possess in charity, I may give up my body to be burnt, but if I have no love, I make nothing of it."

Another sign of the wickedness of these godless workmen is the luxury in which they sometimes live, accumulating wealth as if business were their business. This is far different than John the Baptist, a true minister, who told us that if we had two coats and our neighbor had none, then we must give one to help.

If your ministers do not fully disclose the church's financial affairs on a regular basis, then do not give the wolves in sheep's clothing another cent – and find another church to attend.

Now to clarify an earlier point about tithing: How much should we tithe? The spiritual principles that the old Law of Moses tried to represent will always remain, in this case, giving of ourselves to help worthwhile community service. Under the new covenant, the spirit is our guide, so the answer is that we must give whatever our heart tells us is right. For some of us it might be little or nothing, since if we are poor we do not need to compound the problem. For others, it could be more than 10% of our income, perhaps much more.

But all of this brings up another spiritual lesson that the old law was forerunner to, namely, where to tithe?

The old physical law has all tithes going to the priests, which is what false ministers want, but the new spiritual law shows us that everyone ruled by love is a priest.

This does not mean we should not tithe to church ministers, quite the opposite if you attend a church. But you only need to tithe what you believe is right. The point is that all of us are full-time ministers.

The spirit is our guide for when and how to help in our own ministries, and when it is the lost we aid, they may be curious to understand our motivation. This is our opportunity to share the ageless message of "love one another," even if only by the example of our deed itself.

Lastly, as to the power and lofty stature that these false workmen so often crave, magnifying themselves and/or taking advantage of those who esteem them, I will say only two things. First, it bears repeating what Jesus said, "You will know them by their fruit." Second, remember that every believer reports directly to the spirit of love. No person is in authority over another in the spiritual realm. Be sure any minister you choose to follow or assist understands this, realizing they are only your friend, and not your superior.

Women Ministers

Many churches prohibit or discourage women ministers. They often try to justify this errant behavior by citing the Apostle Paul's teachings. For example: "A woman must listen quietly in church and be perfectly submissive; I allow no woman to teach or dictate to men, she must keep quiet." And again, in another letter he says, "They are not allowed to speak; they must take a subordinate place, as the law enjoins. If they want any information, let them ask their husbands at home; it is disgraceful for a woman to speak in church." The letter then continues by asking, "You challenge this rule? Did God's word start with you?"[1]*

Well, I do challenge that rule. Paul is wrong. And as to the question of with whom did God's word start, I answer by asking if it started for us with Paul or Jesus? Should we teach Christianity or Paulianity?

First, that a woman can instruct men is proved by the fact that not all of the Old Testament era leaders were men. In fact, one leader, namely Deborah, was judge over the entire nation of Israel, and it was through her that the spirit of Jesus chided Barak to follow his orders to go into battle.[2] Would Paul have disobeyed because the rebuke came through a woman?

Second, that a woman may speak in church is proved by the prophetess who scripture records was "never away from the temple... at that very hour she came up and spoke of Him to all."[3] Would Paul have told her she was disgraceful or to "shut-up" as she stood there rejoicing over the infant Jesus? Of course not.

Indeed, Paul even attempts to defend his errant position by claiming "the law enjoins it." In fact, the law does not enjoin it. But rather the "law keepers," that is to say, the Jews of that day, twisted the law in their arrogance and jealously to say that the law that shows differences between the sexes actually shows women to be inferior.

The scriptures do testify that man was created first and woman second, but this is not a statement of worth. Rather, this is simply a point of reference for the spirit to begin teaching our dull minds about love and our creation.

Understand that neither "man" nor "woman" was spiritually first. The spiritual principles that physical man and woman represent (give and receive) occur simultaneously in the pure and perfect spiritual sense. For if receive happens before give, then this is "stealing," a form of violence and a sin. And if give happens without receive happening at the same time, then it would be "force," a form of violence and a sin.

Furthermore, even if Paul did mistakenly believe the Law of Moses enjoined such behavior, that old law is dead now, replaced by a new covenant that is purely spiritual in nature – which is exactly what Paul has argued in other places. He said of the old law that Jesus had "nailed it to the cross," and in another place, "there is no room for male and female, you are all one in Christ Jesus." So we see clearly that Paul has testified against himself on the matter.

But that is not the worst of Paul's mistaken thinking, for after he tells Timothy that women can never teach men and that they must keep quiet, he attempts to justify it by saying, "For Adam was created first, then Eve..." This is true, but so what.

To begin with, how does having been created first merit any special goodness? The other animals were created before Adam, yet he was foremost among them. Consider also that Cain was created, so to speak, before Abel. How can he possibly claim that being first means being superior. No indeed. Adam and Eve were meant to be equals, even though different – and different does not mean inferior.

Paul then continues, saying, "Adam was not deceived, it was Eve who was deceived and fell into sin." Again, this is true, but again it is irrelevant. Paul has totally missed the obvious question: Since Adam and Eve were both of the same flesh, and both had the same sinless spirit within them, what would Adam have done if he were tempted first? The answer, of course, is that Adam would have done the exact same thing! Eve sinned first because she was tempted first.

For the stubborn minded now: Understand Eve was not tempted first because she was weaker, but because she manifests "receive" in the union, which is the only place any entity trying to be seen as "give" could go prior to their separation by this original mistake.

23

Lastly, it is important to remember that the spirit was given to all believers. This is exactly what the true prophecies foretold, and exactly what happened on the Day of Pentecost after Jesus' resurrection. Therefore, the question of whether or not a woman can instruct a man is very clear indeed. The answer is yes, and always has been.

* These verses conclude Chapter 14 of 1st Corinthians. Based on the text, the correct verse order is to relocate verses 37-40 after the first part of verse 33, then follow verse 40 with the remainder of verse 33 and verses 34-36 which brings chapter 14 to a close. If you read the verses I mentioned in their numerical order, and then read them in their correct order, you will see how obvious it is that some scribe altered their original order, and in so doing changed one of Paul's errant opinions into an actual command from the spirit.

Thankfully, the evidence we need to prove this is in verse 37 itself and in verses 38-40 which follow; for it is clear from the text that the command from the Lord is about decorum in the church when believers prophecy or speak in tongues, not about the subordination of women.

More important, we have the spirit itself to prove it, for simply by thinking we come to realize such a self-evident truth. We all had mothers who taught us! A man does not grow from childhood into adulthood to find himself not only equal to, but spiritually superior to his mother. However, he may come to see the subtle differences, generally speaking, between their genders, as a daughter may learn similar things from watching her father. All will be blessed for the increased knowledge.

Of course, this rearrangement of Paul's words was easy to do since it fit right in with his other incorrect teachings about women, teachings that differ vastly from what Jesus taught and what some true prophecies foresaw.

Jesus never commanded such behavior towards women. He could not have because it would be contrary to what he previously taught in person.

Long before that, Deborah judged the entire nation of Israel. When Jesus was a baby, a woman prophesied at the temple in Jerusalem in front of him and his parents. These things happened under the old physical law. How much more would such things be welcome under the new covenant of spiritual law? Welcome indeed! This fact is proved by the spirit itself, for we know that it was given to "all who were gathered" on Pentecost – male and female alike. Jesus told us, "The flesh profits nothing." Clearly then, the spirit never told Paul that women could not teach, could not speak in church, and must be subordinate. Just as clear is that the Apostle's teachings about women are often wrong.

Finally, since it is clear in much of Paul's writing that he is trying to follow the spirit of love, how is it that he went astray regarding women?

In my opinion, Paul is turned aside from the true way because of the incredible hardness of the people's hearts, just as Moses turned aside when he permitted divorce, and again when the people's wickedness made him doubt at Meribah. I think Paul was intimidated by society as it was, therefore he allowed the status quo to continue, rather than face the hostile reaction he would get from so many men if he ever told them plainly that their women, though different, were equal. But by never losing sight of the most important thing – teaching the people to "love one another" – he knew all else would have to follow in time, even if it took a little longer.

Holy Days

In the Law of Moses, holy days are a physical representation of the still forming spiritual world of a coming christ.

Before talking about these holy days, which are of minor interest at most, it is important to note these days are no longer in effect, since the christ Jesus has begun a new covenant. This new covenant is purely spiritual in nature and has only one commandment: "Love one another," a commandment so profound it can only be written on our hearts.

Some churches teach that believers are still obligated to keep these days, but they are as far astray as churches who teach that Easter and Christmas are holy.

They often try to justify their error by citing certain scriptures. For example, when Moses commanded the Israelites to observe these days, he said that they were "permanent statutes." Also, the Apostle Paul sometimes observed these days depending on what church he was visiting at the time. In addition, Paul once wrote, "Everyone must be convinced in his own mind; the man who values a particular day does so to the Lord." Let us examine these things, starting with Paul's position.

Admittedly, Paul tolerated some congregations to continue observing days, but his letters show he discouraged it regularly and never instituted it among any congregations. And as far as Paul celebrating these days, that was purely incidental to his attending Jewish/Israelite festivals to spread the news that their christ had indeed finally come.

Paul understood the Law of Moses served only as physical representation of spiritual ideals, which are now here in their fullness for some of us as manifested in the christ Jesus. Of course, the highest spiritual ideal contained in the old holy days is that every day is a holy day, because every day is to be without sin. But all of this is moot now, since the old law is dead. This is why, in arguing against the old law, Paul said of Jesus, "He canceled the regulations that stood against us – all these obligations he set aside when he nailed them to the cross."

And again, in another letter, he wrote this very sharp rebuke to a church interested in keeping the law of the old covenant, saying, "I simply want to ask you one thing: Did you receive the spirit by doing what the law commands or by believing the gospel message? Are you such fools: Did you begin with the spirit only to end now with the flesh?"[1]

So we see Paul's true feelings on the matter clearly. He tolerates observing the old holy days in the already established Jewish churches, but discourages it as having become needless, and forbids such things in all the new churches he is shepherding.

Now as for Moses saying these holy day observances were "permanent statutes," that is true. But what happens when the spirit of Jesus, who gave the ideas in the law to Moses in the first place, says that the old law is finished? Obviously, that law is dead. And this is precisely what has happened, for a true prophesy says this very thing: "A day comes, the Eternal promises, when I make a fresh compact with all the house of Israel – not like the compact I once made with their fathers, the day I took them by the hand to bring them out of Egypt's land... this is the compact I make with Israel in the end; I will put my law within them, writing it on their hearts."[2] And when Jesus completed his work (having ascended and sent back the spirit to help), this new covenant was complete.

Having said all this, we can now take a look at the old Law of Moses, Sabbaths, special Sabbaths, and special observances.

Please note that the special Sabbaths, of which there are seven each year, are called by a variety of names. They include "great" days, "high" days, or they were sometimes just called the Sabbath, like the regular seventh day observance was called.

A good way to visualize these days is to look at them on a calendar. I have reconstructed a partial calendar from the year Jesus was crucified to picture them and included it at the end of this chapter. Only the 1st, 3rd, and 7th months are shown, as they are all that are necessary.

Also, for those of you unfamiliar with this subject, the Jews did not use the Julian calendar that most of the Roman Empire used to chart the days (until around 1582 when it was replaced by the Gregorian calendar we still use today). Instead, the Jews of that day used a lunar calendar that marked the beginning of each year around the vernal equinox (the beginning of Spring). It consisted of alternating 30 day months, and 29 day months, for a total of 354 days per year. Since this would quickly make the seasons out of line with the solar year of 365-1/4 days, they added an additional month to their calendar as needed, approximately every 3 years. This kept the holy days relatively stationary, so they always happened at the same general time each year.

As you look at the calendar and the brief summary of regular Sabbaths, "great/high day" Sabbaths, and special observances, remember that the Jews measured a day from sunset to sunset. Therefore, each day on this calendar would end at sunset, having begun on the preceding day at sunset. For example: The paschal lambs were always slain in the afternoon of the 14th day of the first month of the year (on the Jewish calendar), and the Passover supper was eaten by all of Israel just before the sun set. After the supper, when the sun sets, the 14th day is ended and the 15th day begins. Under the old Judaic law, which was also called the Law of Moses, this 15th day is the First Day of Unleavened Bread, the first of the 7 annual high holy days.

Here is a brief overview of all the Old Testament holy days and commemorative events. Note that I used the English names of the days to make the calendar that follows easier to understand. I call the first day of the week Sunday, the second day Monday, etc.

Seventh Day Sabbath

These were the regular holy days, observed on the last day of every week. "During six days work may be done, but on the seventh day, there is to be a Sabbath of entire rest, and a sacred gathering..."

Passover

This was not a holy day, but rather a holy event, the first of two each year. It was commemorative of the miracle that led to the Israelite exodus from the bondage of physical slavery to Egypt. "On the fourteenth day of the first month towards evening, the Passover of the Eternal begins."

Days of Unleavened Bread (Festival of Unleavened Bread)

A special seven day period that opened and closed with a "high" holy day. "On the fifteenth day of the same month the festival of unleavened bread in honor of the Eternal begins: for seven days you must eat unleavened bread. On the first day of the festival you must hold a sacred gathering...and on the seventh day you must hold another sacred gathering."

First Fruits Wave Offering

This was not a holy day, but rather another holy event, the second of two each year. It was commemorative of the future miracle (the coming christ Jesus) that would lead to his world's exodus from the bondage of spiritual slavery to sin. "You shall bring a sheaf from the first fruits of your harvest to the priest, who shall wave the sheaf to and fro before the Eternal, that you may be accepted; he shall wave it on the day after the Sabbath. On the day you wave the sheaf, you must offer an unblemished male lamb as a burnt offering to the Eternal...until you have brought the offering for your God you must eat neither bread nor grain" (from any new harvest of the new year).

Day of Pentecost (Feast of First Fruits)

This was a "high" holy day. "You bring the sheaf of the waved offering, you shall count seven full weeks, fifty days to the day...and on that day you shall proclaim a sacred gathering."

Days of Trumpets

This was a "high" holy day. "On the first day of the seventh month you must hold as an entire rest, a day of remembrance accompanied by trumpet blasts, and a sacred gathering..."

Day of Atonement

This was a "high" holy day. "On the tenth day of this month, however, which is Expiation day, you must hold a sacred gathering; you must abstain and fast..."

Days of Booths and Last Great Day

A special seven day period that opened with a "high" holy day, and when the seven days ended, was immediately followed by another "high" holy day. "On the fifteenth day of this seventh month the festival of booths begins, for seven days, in honor of the Eternal. On the first day there shall be a sacred gathering...and on the eighth day you shall hold a sacred gathering..."

Here is a question: Were all of these seven high holy days and the holy observances/events fulfilled in the same year?

Obviously, the two holy observances/events happened in the same year, for Jesus was crucified on Passover and ascended to the Father when the First Fruits Wave Offering took place. Also certain is that the first three of the seven high holy days have been fulfilled. The first two of these are the First and Seventh Day of Unleavened Bread, symbolic of our creation and God's resting afterwards. The third of the seven is the Day of Pentecost, symbolic of receiving the spirit of love, which came to us shortly after Jesus died and arose.

What about the other four high holy days? Were they fulfilled in the same year?

The answer as I see it is yes. Just before his execution, Jesus asked his father that he be "spared this cup if it were possible." He also once said, "All things are possible for them that believe." Pause for moment and consider the implications in those two comments by Jesus...! In addition, shortly before Jesus was led away to execution, he told his disciples "From now on you see the Father." These are also extremely important words from Jesus. Lastly, we have the example of Isaac the son being spared by Abraham the father.

To put this all another way, a key of any christ is the leap of one's essence from the temporary physical realm into the eternal spiritual realm. So the other holy days, by definition, become purely spiritual immediately after the Day of Pentecost was fulfilled. In short, in the new covenant Jesus wisely allows the whole spirit to help us in place of just himself. His selfishness has been subdued, and the authority of love, which he has been following, has been rightly elevated to his supreme guide. We all need to be the same way in this regard.

However, since some would endlessly argue "no" to my point of view, I will suggest an alternative answer to the question of whether all the holy days were fulfilled, which is: "It is not important."

Why unimportant? The answer is because if we truly accept the authority of the spirit of love, anything remaining from the former physical law is by definition irrelevant.

As to the plethora of new holy days that sprang up among the gentiles, all are meaningless from the start.

For example, look at Christmas. This day is celebrated as the day Jesus was born, but the date of his birth is unknown.

Many of the early Christian churches invented holy days, their twisted reasoning being that it would help the spread of Christianity to have their own celebrations whenever there was a traditional pagan festival. Hence, we have Christmas at the winter solstice, which was December 25 on the Roman Empire's calendar that was used in those days.

In short, this day, and all other Christian so called holy days are pure fiction, marketing decisions at heart, concocted by parasites that took control of Jesus' legacy and turned it into a business.

In fact, Christmas is a relatively late-in-coming artificial holy day, since early church records have absolutely no record of this festival, though other man-made holy days and observances were already in place. Today, however, the celebration of Christmas has become so widespread that many people truly believe it is really a special day, and have never once heard that it originated from pagan festivals at the winter solstice.

Does all of this mean that we cannot enjoy Christmas festivities? Not at all. But true religion is simply loving one another and is not contained in any ritual or tradition, no matter how wise it appears on the outside. If we want to follow a particular tradition, in this case giving gifts or sending cards, that is just fine, if your heart is in it. But proclaiming the day as Jesus' birthday is senseless because no one knows when that was. More importantly, even if we did know the day we could not ascribe any holiness to it, since every other day is just as valuable.

Again, the spirit reveals that every day is a holy day, for every day should be without sin.

The so-called holy days of Easter Sunday and Good Friday are more Christian mythology. In fact, not only did the earliest churches never celebrate such a tradition, Easter was derived from a pagan festival held during the vernal equinox and devoted to a fertility idol.

Did Jesus die on a Friday afternoon and was he resurrected on the following Sunday morning?" That answer is an emphatic "No." Jesus said about his death, "the Son of Man will be three days and three nights in the heart of the earth."[3] This is about 72 hours and is not even close to the day and a half that most preachers expound. Jesus died and was resurrected three days and nights later – just like he said would happen.

In fact, we can actually see when everything took place by examining the four gospel accounts, then putting all the facts together. (But first we will need to address one minor point on which the four gospel accounts are in disagreement. And before we do that, we need to look at how the first three gospels evolved.)

To begin with, Mark wrote an account of Jesus' life and teachings many years after the events. He was witness to none of the events he described. As time went on his written record was copied over and over and passed along to different churches. During this period, many other teachings of Jesus, whether true or false, in whole or in part, passed from person to person orally. It soon followed that other Christians would construct newer written records that were more complete. Luke and the author of the book titled Matthew simply used versions of Mark's account as a blueprint to incorporate their own expanded narratives.

The reason I am spending some time on the origin of the first three gospels is because they disagree with John's version of the events, not about what happened, but rather when things happened. The Apostle John's version of when these events happened is correct, while the others do not match his account on one particular point. Some might want to argue that it is "three against one" as regards the point of conflict. What I have shown here is that it is really only "one against one," since Luke and the author of Matthew simply copied this portion of Mark's version into their own words and in so doing made the same mistake.

The following verses are from Bible books of Matthew, Mark, Luke and John:

Matthew 26:17

"On the first day of unleavened bread, the disciples came up and said to him, 'Where do you want us to prepare for you to eat the Passover?'"

Mark 14:12

"On the first day of unleavened bread, the day when the paschal lamb was sacrificed, the disciples said to him, 'Where do you want us to go prepare for you to eat the Passover?'"

Luke 22:7-9

"Then came the day of unleavened bread, when the paschal lamb had to be sacrificed. So Christ dispatched Peter and John, saying, 'Go and prepare the Passover for us to eat.' They asked him, 'Where do you want us to prepare it?'"

John 13:1

"Now before the Passover festival Christ knew that the time had come for him to pass from this world to the Father."

John's account after this verse shows the sequence of events that followed and makes it clear that this night "before" Passover was Jesus' last before being crucified.

As we look at the comparison, we see the disagreement between John's account and the others. But not only is this part of the books of Matthew and Luke simply a rewording of Mark's account, all three make a statement that is impossible. All claim that Jesus is going to eat the Passover on the First Day of Unleavened Bread, but these are two different days. The Passover is always eaten at the end of the day, shortly before nightfall. After sunset is when the First Day of Unleavened Bread begins. A minor point, but any citizen from the area would know the difference, and so would anyone who was an eyewitness. But John is a resident of that region. And John is an eyewitness to the events. Furthermore, John is a disciple, an original Apostle. He therefore is absolutely familiar with the special observances and holy days of the Jews. So who has the facts straight as to when everything happened, Mark or John?

33

And if you think about John's version of when everything took place, and how Jesus and his disciples were eating the Passover meal before the rest of Israel would on the next day, it makes perfect sense. Jesus himself is the Passover sacrifice for his whole world on the next day.

There are more proofs as well: The Pharisees said of putting Jesus to death, "It must not be during the festival; that would mean a popular riot."[4] Both Mark and the author of Matthew made this statement in their accounts, but the festival begins on the First Day of Unleavened Bread, which is the day they said Jesus was arrested and crucified. Obviously, they confused when things happened, having been more concerned about what happened.

And in Luke's errant account we find one of the strongest proofs for John's version. He states that the two Apostles Jesus sent to prepare the Passover for him were Peter and John.[5] Since John is the very person who is preparing the meal, it makes sense to believe his account of the events that shows Jesus ate the Passover a day early.

Lastly, the scriptures record the Pharisees wanted Jesus' and the two criminals' legs broken to hasten their deaths, because "it was a day of preparation... for that Sabbath was a great day.[6] (A day of preparation is any day immediately before a Sabbath.)

Notice the coming Sabbath was a "great day" Sabbath. Only seven of these happen in each year, and the first one was always the First Day of Unleavened Bread. This is positive proof that Jesus was crucified on Passover.

But when was Jesus resurrected? It was three days and three nights later, just like he said.

We know from the scriptures Jesus died at "about the ninth hour" by the old methods of telling what time of day it was. This translates to about 3:00 p.m. as we tell time today. This means we can add 72 hours and almost pinpoint the time he was resurrected. When Mary arrived at the tomb Jesus had already been resurrected since around 3:00 p.m. the previous afternoon! Nobody knew it because the day he rose was a regular 7th day Sabbath. All his followers were still keeping the commandment to rest and refrain from working on the Sabbath. But early on the first day of the week Mary came to the tomb with the burial spices she had prepared and made the great discovery.

Some might have some question as to why Jesus did not go tell his disciples he was resurrected as soon as it happened. The answer is that since it was the Sabbath he was still observing the day of rest himself, for he had not yet ascended to the Father.

Others might ask why Mary did not come to the tomb with her burial spices sooner than she did? The answer cannot be certain and one would think she would have known Nicodemus took care of this matter. Perhaps she simply went to the tomb to mourn and we are the victims of more creative writing in those papers we call scripture. Assuming though, that her actions were historical fact, logic provides a very probable conjecture if we examine the scriptural accounts and remember the customs of that time.

The Law of Moses forbids any work to be done on any Sabbath. The Sabbaths occurred on the seventh day of each week and on seven other special days each year. A "day of preparation" was the day before any of these Sabbaths. In general, these preparation days were very hectic as any time-sensitive work projects would need to be finished by sunset, the next day being unavailable to complete them. The day the Passover event was held was also always a day of preparation, because the Sabbath of the First Day of Unleavened Bread always follows. But extremely little regular work would get done on this one particular preparation day each year. This is because the Passover celebration was a very big event in the Jewish community in Jesus' time, and every family was expected to partake in the ritual, which required extensive preparation in itself.

Jesus died shortly before the Passover supper. The sunset came soon after this, which marked the beginning of the First Day of Unleavened Bread, and all work had to stop. After this Sabbath, Mary would have used the "common" day that followed to prepare things for her own household, since this day was yet another "day of preparation," for the regular 7th day Sabbath was coming the very next day. In short, this particular preparation day would have been exceedingly busy for her, as she tried to catch up from yesterday while preparing for tomorrow.

So we see that following Passover, three full days – a great day Sabbath, a day of preparation, and a 7th day Sabbath – took place before Mary could go to the tomb. Then she had to wait a little longer, until sunrise of the next day in order to have sufficient light to work and hopefully find nearby help to roll away the stone.

Lastly, why did Jesus not ascend to his Father on the day he was resurrected? This is because "all things written about the Son of Man in the Law, the Prophets, and the Psalms must be fulfilled,"([7] as Jesus himself said. This being the case, he could not ascend until the high priest performed the "first fruits wave offering." Historically, this was always done on the first day of the first new week following Passover. And the scriptures tell us how Jesus told Mary to leave and go tell his brothers that he was "ascending to my Father and yours, to my God and yours."

1st Month

Sun.	Mon.	Tue.	Wed.	Thur.	Fri.	Sat.
				1	2	3
4	5	6	7	8	9	10
11	12	13	14 Passover Supper	15 1st Day of Unleavened Bread	16	17
18 1st Fruits Wave Offering	19	20	21 7th Day of Unleavened Bread	22	23	24
25	26	27	28	28	30	

3rd Month

Sun.	Mon.	Tue.	Wed.	Thur.	Fri.	Sat.
1	2	3	4	5	6	7
8 Pentecost	9	10	11	12	13	14
15	16	17	18	19	20	21
22	23	24	25	26	27	28
29	30					

7th Month

Sun.	Mon.	Tue.	Wed.	Thur.	Fri.	Sat.
						1 Day of Trumpets
2	3	4	5	6	7	8
9	10 Day of Atonement	11	12	13	14	15 1st Day of Booths
16	17	18	19	20	21	22 Last Great Day
23/30	24	25	26	27	28	29

Jesus' Death and Resurrection

	Wed.	Thur.	Fri.	Sat.	Sun.
12:00 am					
1:00 am					
2:00 am					
3:00 am					
4:00 am					
5:00 am					
6:00 am					Jesus appears to Mary
7:00 am					
8:00 am					
9:00 am	Jesus crucified				Wave Offering & Jesus' Ascension
10:00 am					
11:00 am					
12:00 am					
1:00 pm					
2:00 pm					
3:00 pm	Jesus dies			Jesus resurrected	
4:00 pm					
5:00 pm	Passover				
6:00 pm					
* 7:00 pm	1st Day of Unleavened Bread Sabbath begins		Regular Sabbath begins		
8:00 pm					
9:00 pm					
10:00 pm					
11:00 pm					

* The Jewish day was from sunset to sunset, approximately 7:00 pm in early spring

40

We Are Gods

The creation itself shows us that we are already a part of something that is greater than ourselves, and that we can grow to become just like it. Simple examples would be how some acorns become oak trees and some caterpillars become butterflies.

Do you know we are gods? This is what the scriptures teach us, though we seldom hear it from the pulpit. In fact, many preachers teach the very opposite, saying we are not and never will be. Such ministers have not understood the scriptures very well because the evidence is overwhelming.

To begin with, before creating us, God said: "Let us make man in our own image." What could be clearer than this! There are many more proofs in the scriptures that we are gods.

For instance, when the Pharisees challenge Jesus for saying he was God's son, he rebukes them by replying that it was written in the law that we are all gods.[1] And from the Psalms, written of our need to repent from sin and turn to his ways: "Though you are gods, all sons of the Most High, yet, like mere men, you shall die, you shall perish like a demon."[2]

Here is yet another enlightening scripture: "We had fathers of our flesh to discipline us, and we yielded to them. Shall we not far more submit to the father of our spirits, and so live?"[3]

David saw all this; and what did he say of it? He burst into song, declaring, "I thank thee with all my heart, I sing thy praise in face of all the Gods." Then closing the same song, he sings, "Eternal One, thy kindness never fails, thou wilt not drop the work thou hast begun." So, indeed, even though we sinned, God is making us into his own image – he has not changed his mind.

Jesus told us about it himself when he said, "Whatever the father does, the son also does the same," and "If you remain in me and my words remain in you, then ask whatever you like and you shall have it."

Lastly, consider these amazing words, also from Jesus: "If you had faith the size of a mustard seed...nothing would be impossible for you." Truly, anyone for whom anything is possible is a god indeed!

In fact, we are already so powerful that not only our prayers, but even our thoughts are sometimes brought to life by the spirit, often without our realizing it.

Marriage in Heaven

Jesus said, "When people rise from the dead, they neither marry nor are married, they are like the angels in heaven."

Does this mean that you would not be best friends with your beloved in the next age, if you both desire it? Not at all, for Jesus is speaking only of physical marriage, not spiritual union.

Consider what John the Baptist said of Jesus: "He who has the bride is the bridegroom, the bridegroom's friend, who stands listening to him, is heartily glad at the sound of the bridegroom's voice. Such is my joy, and it is complete." So there is a bride and a marriage, spiritually speaking.

 Jesus assured us that, "if two of you agree on earth about anything, it will be done for you by my father in heaven." Therefore, if a couple who are only physically married desire earnestly to be spiritually married, they will be, as simple as that.

More noteworthy is that Jesus uses marriage more than once to describe what heaven is like. "The realm of heaven," he said, "may be compared to a king who gave a marriage banquet..." And in another place, Jesus said, "Then shall the realm of heaven be compared to ten maidens who took their lamps and went out to meet the bridegroom and the bride."[1]

Note that the words "and the bride" are missing in many of the ancient manuscripts which were in turn used for most of the modern translations. Since the words are a perfect fit with the spirit of love, the early omissions are the result of tampering. I would also add that it appeals to a selfish man that he should have a multitude of wives, yet those women may only have him.

In marriage, Solomon was not blessed for his multitude of carnal unions, but he was blessed for the one companion who loved him without reservation. Speaking of him in a mighty parable, his true soul mate, the queen of his heart rejoiced, "Maidens of Zion, come, look at my king, crowned by his mother, the day of his marriage, the day of his rapture."[2]

Eternal Hell

Do the wicked really go to a place of fire to writhe in endless agony forever and ever? Absolutely not, and the mere idea of such a thing is a vulgar obscenity to the spirit.

This fictional concept was created many centuries ago by greedy priests to terrify the laity, thereby suspending their common sense and logical reasoning. The church's goal, of course, was the people's submission to priestly authority and acceptance of their twisted message. It continues to exist in the doctrines of many churches today, for the same reason, and also because some people have no taste for mercy or forgiveness.

This is not to say that eternal punishment does not exist in a sense, but what it entails is not so endlessly hateful.

Pause a moment and reflect on the difference between punishment and punishing.

We came into being by the power of God, and that power is love, and so it is love that sustains us. Are we to believe that the power of love will eternally sustain someone's existence on the one hand so it can forever torture them on the other hand? The whole idea of eternal hell collapses in its absurdity.

Eternal punishing is crazy because it would mean that love is unforgiving and sadistic. Love is endless mercies and eventual forgiveness for anything – always. Be warned though, this is not to say that those who rejected the authority of love will not suffer the harvest of pain and destruction that they sowed, for indeed they will. This is the second death in the place called the lake of fire.

And yet, even so, the spirit in its infinite love will someday save those who do die and perish in unbelief, for the lake of fire is only a parable for living with death in our future. Therefore, if someone dies without having submitted to the authority of love, they will simply find themselves consigned to the prison of life in a mortal form again. That next age will be a new world for them, and nothing will have survived from their past, not a single memory, except their final thought, from the heart, which will be, "I am nothing."

Fortunately, this tragic final admission draws the spirit's attention. For this life and the punishment that results from not using it properly is as angry as a loving god gets with his disobedient children. By a god's very nature they are simply unable to allow any of us to die and suffer forever.

Love always triumphs.

It is for this reason, though every hateful spirit will be dead and gone, the spirit of God in its overwhelming love and mercy relents. Solomon says that God will "bring back whatever is lost." The commitment of the spirit to love is so profound, so eternal, it says of love's authority, "Every knee shall bow" and "Every tongue confess." And we know that such honesty by a demon always catches the spirit's notice, and that any good thing will eventually lead to life. No one will be left out forever.

In fact, we actually see mercy for spirits who are still dead forming in advance, when Jesus told us the parable of the rich man in torment, while the beggar he ignored was in comfort. Jesus said that some spirits in Paradise wanted to cross over and help.[1] Since it is always lawful to do good, and compassion is very good indeed, God will one day allow their crossing into the abyss to help.

When will that day be? Only at the beginning of a new age, when all members of the next christ want to help, for there must be complete unity and agreement among all members of the spirit in order to cross into the abyss. This cannot happen until every tear of the newborn is wiped away and forgotten, erased by the joy of their togetherness. The misery they suffered at the hands of those they now intend to help will be counted as forgiven, as they themselves were once forgiven.

So we see that eternal punishment is in the form of missing an opportunity that can never be regained, until the consequence of neglecting it is incurred. That consequence, for those who refused the authority of love, is death, and they will have forever missed salvation – at this time.

And knowing that another chance will someday come in another age will be of no solace at all for those who rejected the authority of love.

They must perish into nothingness, while people they once knew rejoice with each other and possess happiness beyond comprehension, each actually saying of themselves: "I am." Meanwhile, the final words of the lost as they die their second death (spiritually) will be "I am nothing," and this will happen at the very feet of those they once despised.

Does this mean that Jesus comes to die again? Not at all. A new christ comes for a new world, and that will be each of us someday, if we have not already done so, or are not already in the process.

We see this clearly when the next christ (that spoke to the Apostle John in the book of Revelations) says to any believer at the end of that age, "I will be his God, and he shall be my son."[2] And so again, a christ is keeping his promise to give his loved ones all that is his, just as his father gave everything to him.

So now we see our future, present, or past. Every newborn sinless child of god one day enters the abyss, just as Jesus did, declaring "Let there be light," which is an analogy for giving love. And as proof of the eternal spark of life (love) that this new christ now has inherent, they resolve to make those among the lost that are repentant into their own image (spiritually), as their parents did for them.

We even know who some of the elect will be in the next age, for Jesus said that some of those in torment with the rich man wanted to cross over as well.

The Trinity

Some people try to describe God as a "trinity." This confusing description stems from three of the different ways that Christian scriptures describe the embodiment of love – Jesus, God, and the Spirit.

Rather than a trinity, a much clearer picture is seen by describing God in just two different ways: as one individual and also as infinite individuals.

To explain briefly, there is an infinite number of beings (the "from everlasting") all of whom can call themselves "God" (individually), and they live together in sinlessness and collectively comprise what we know as the spirit.

This collective group calls itself "one God" when an individual member identifies itself to a dead spirit, a symbol of the perfect unity the member is a part of. And a christ is simply a new sinless god, the newest member of this "from everlasting" spirit, the baby as it were.

This perfect oneness of infinite members is the result of love shared without measure by all the members. Indeed, love is the eternal life sustaining force of all these members, just as blood is the life sustaining force in our physical realm.

Here are a number of other related things in hopes to make it clearer. To begin with, just as the christ Jesus had a God, so it is that Jesus' God was once a christ and had a god, and that god was formerly a christ who had a god, ad infinitum.

Realize that everyone is going to be a christ, a savior for a world someday (their own world), if they have not already done so, or are not presently in the process.

It is true, and scripture affords this excellent proof when a christ reveals to the Apostle John that the time will come when that christ will "make all things new." The spirit then continues, saying of any who conquered (the authority of unloving spirits on their behaviors), "I will be his God, and he shall be my son."

David saw this and said, "The Lord said to my Lord, 'Sit at my right hand until I make your enemies a footstool for your feet.' "[1] Zechariah saw something similar and said "even the lame on that day shall be like David himself, and David's house shall be like God himself."[2]

Consider also the testimony that Jesus himself gives of his origin. When he was in spirit as one with the Infinite, he said of himself, "I am the Eternal," and "I am from everlasting to everlasting," and that he has "no beginning of days and no end of days." But when he came in the flesh, partly away from his father and mother, and the other members of the spirit, his testimony is far different.

In fact, Jesus actually rejected a compliment from a man that sincerely called him "good," saying in reply, "Why call me good, no one is good, no one but God."

How can he say that?

Jesus says this because when he is apart from the collective spirit, which is comprised of his father and mother, and all of the other infinite number of gods, his own righteousness only begins at the start of his new world. That is the new world they began creating when they entered the abyss to give life to the dead in the void by the power of love. (The word "they" is used to make clear this entity is spiritually "give and receive" at all times. They are also one entity that was physically "give and receive" before and especially after life in this flesh. Though this future physical form is not a thing we can comprehend very well, for the caterpillar cannot fully envision how the butterfly it will become will look, until the metamorphosis happens.)

Do you realize that you will be like your god someday? Indeed, some are so far beyond this that they no longer consider themselves anything but a member of the spirit.

Such a design for these spiritual things is easy to see in the physical framework. Just look at life itself. For example: First, a seed becomes a fetus in the womb. Then it is born an infant into a new world, but the placenta it was attached to and received nourishment from is discarded. Then that child one day becomes a parent itself, then grandparent, great-grandparent, and so on.

Likewise, love is the spiritual seed that begets goodness to grow within us, here in the womb of this earthly life. When we die here, it is simply our spiritual birth as a new child into a new world, while our body here is discarded, just as our placenta once was.

Will we also be a parent someday in that new spiritual realm? Of course. Jesus said that his father has given him all things, and that he intends to do the same for us, spiritually speaking. My own dad told me how his father found ways to bless him, and I see how my dad did the same for me. I have tried to do the same for my son, and know you have for your children. If mere mortals do this in our crippled physical realm, then how much more will our spiritual parents bless us in a place without sin!

Are we really to think that the One that calls itself the Eternal is making something into its own image for the first, last, and only time in all eternity? Of course not, and this is why Solomon said of God's design, "Whatever is, it has already been; whatever is to be, already is; and God is forever bringing back what disappears."

Lastly, God himself spoke from heaven in response to Jesus telling him to glorify his name, saying, "I have glorified my name, and I will glorify it again." [3]

Those words signify Jesus' own spiritual children someday, as Jesus was a child to his spiritual father, though he never doubted for a moment, so the voice only benefited the dead with Jesus who heard it.

The voice also reveals a mote in God's eye, for the "from everlasting" had no need to speak aloud to Jesus. I mention it only to show how every member of the spirit is always growing and learning. Also, it is important to note that depending on where you are spiritually, the voice could be more friend than enemy. But if you are ruled by the authority of love, such a voice has to be more demon than love. Note I said "could" be a friend earlier. Any directions to do harm to other individuals in any way is far more demon than god indeed. Compare the childish spirit of Jesus in the Old Testament instructing the Israelites to kill enemies, as opposed to the new covenant of the mature Jesus telling us to "love one another."

A God Grows Up

David wrote of his own blessing, and also about the coming christ, saying, "You are now my son, this day I am your father."[1] The scriptures reveal many interesting concepts, and one of them is how young gods grow up. In physical terms it might be described as conception leading to birth, or a child becoming an adult.

When the spirit of Jesus was young and not yet fully mature, he spoke to the patriarchs, Moses, and prophets through his spirit and angels, in an effort to wake us up to the joy that could be ours. This was a joy that he possessed and considered sharing, though he understood little about it. But when he was more fully mature, and all things were ready, then he himself was sent to display the even greater wisdom of the spirit which he now much better understood, and which he now truly desired to share.

We can see the contrast between childish and mature by comparing the time of Moses against Jesus' teachings when he dwelt in the flesh. For example, the immature spirit of Jesus tells Moses, "Thou shall not kill," but then leads the Israelites in war against various inhabitants in the land of Canaan. But when the mature spirit comes in the flesh as Jesus, we are told, "Turn the other cheek" and "Love one another."

In another example, his spirit tells his prophets that "his name shall be great," and that he intends to "get glory for himself." But the mature spirit of this christ, personified in Jesus, expresses his concern for his father's name and recognition.

Here are a few of the last words in the Bible (spoken about a new age): "I will be his God and he shall be my son." This saying represents yet another cycle of lost souls who will be conceived by the spirit of love. This is also an analogy of the growth of Jesus, who passed from spiritual childhood to adulthood when he was willing to give his life for the love he believes in. He trusted in his father that by the power of the spirit of love they share in, the essence of who he is would rise again. And indeed it has, even more, for Jesus is now passing from spiritual adulthood to spiritual fatherhood, for the speaker of this quote ("I will be his God and he shall be my son") is not the christ Jesus, who has now attained the knowledge and rank this quote promises others. Rather, the speaker is a future coming christ, for John's revelations can never be applicable to those of us who are already ruled by the authority of the spirit of love. We report directly to the spirit of god within us now, so any prophecy is false. "The old wine is good enough" is what we will rightly say if those future days appear to come to us.

It was not without reason that Jesus said it was "easier for heaven and earth to pass away than for an iota of the law to fail." The fact is heaven and earth did pass away! The scriptures record that at the very moment Jesus died there was an earthquake and many of the dead were resurrected. But how can this be? Jesus said he was the "resurrection and life," but the fact remains that Jesus does not rise for three days – how can the dead rise before the christ Jesus who is a first-born son of God?

The answer to how this is all possible is a difficult concept to explain, so it would be too much of a digression to talk more about it here. Succeeding chapters about time and reality will hopefully help make it clearer, but I am leaving it to the spirit to answer that question in detail, for this resurrection has to do with the spiritually dead who awoke to the living example of the future bride of the christ Jesus. Also, understand this resurrection of many of the dead was purely spiritual, for witnesses only saw apparitions.

In conclusion, we can indeed see the spirit of Jesus is growing. When he spoke to the prophets, saying, "I am always the same," and "I never change," he was only speaking of the virtues of the spirit which are a part of him, for love and the fruits of the spirit will always be the same. But as for himself, he will always be learning and growing, as will all of us, for growing forever is how it must be in a world where death has no power.

So the christ called Jesus, who was the son and who has become like his heavenly father, will eventually grow to see himself as just another member of the spirit, just another member of the "from everlasting." And Jesus and his bride, and their father and mother, and their father and mother (and on and on forever) live in utter equality with absolutely no distinctions of rank or worth among members. For the virtues of the spirit of love are ultimately the only real god to all these infinite number of

51

members of the spirit, all of whom independently possess life inherent and bear the name of "God."

This means that real religion, the proper worship of god, is simply the practice of all of the fruits of the spirit of love with unity and goodwill towards all other life.

The Law Fails

If we look back at the old covenant Law of Moses we see that a situation could arise, or a hypothetical case could be invented, by which every law would find an occasion to be righteously disregarded.

This is why David was able to eat the consecrated bread that was only lawful for the Levitical priests, and again, this is why Aaron was able to abstain from eating the high priest's sin-offering on the day two of his sons died. "The law was made for man, not man for the law."

The fact that the Law of Moses might be disregarded on some occasions proves that it was fallible and destined to wear out, though it does not mean that the law was unrighteous. It simply shows that the law was only temporary, a counselor for the behavior of our dead but awakening souls during our spiritual infancy, until we were ready for adult things, namely, the law of love. This new law is brought to us by the spirit and was demonstrated by Jesus (and a multitude of others both before and since).

The concept of the law overall can be seen by comparing it to the way our physical parents set down rules for us during our youth. To disobey them usually resulted in their being angry and perhaps our getting punished as well. But when we grew older, the rules they set down were no longer needed to teach and protect us, often no longer sensible, and so they passed away having accomplished their intended purpose. So we see the Law of Moses does wear out and fail in this way, for to make adults obey childhood rules would be wrong indeed.

Jesus said, "It is easier for heaven and earth to pass away than for an iota of the law to lapse." This is true of course, but understand that Jesus is not saying it cannot happen, only how difficult it would be. This is important because several of these laws were on the verge of failing, owing to the spiritual growth of some of the people. A few of these laws would have failed very soon if Jesus had not come to end the childhood rule of the law by giving us the adult covenant of love, that lasts forever.

Of all the rules in the law which were close to wearing out and thereby failing, there is one that stands out all alone. This is the rule about divorce. This is the statute in which Moses permitted a man to divorce his wife by simply giving her a letter of dismissal.

The Pharisees saw this weakness too, and so they tried to trap Jesus by asking him his opinion on this rule, hoping he would agree with it. But Jesus rebuked them since it was never his will, saying, "Moses permitted you to divorce your wives on account of the hardness of your hearts, but it was not so from the beginning." Then continuing, he stated, "I tell you, whoever divorces his wife except for adultery and marries another woman, commits adultery."

Other laws were also close to being outgrown, and therefore passing away, since Jesus shows us a better way than Moses ever understood on many points. But the law on divorce had failed, spiritually speaking.

That something in the law should fail spiritually is a landmark moment for us. It represents Adam and Eve (or any other true husband and wife) having their first real spark of forgiveness for each other since their fall and separation. In short, it represents their first real growth of love for each other. Seriously considering forgiveness, they actually accepted each other again as equals, for a moment. Baby's first steps, as it were.

This is the reason Jesus came when he did.

Mistakes

The spirit of love within us is our guide. It helps us interpret what is right and wrong behavior, and we somehow inherently understand we should try to be guided by this inner voice of love. Occasionally, we really do not know how to behave, and in these cases it is best to treat others as we would like to be treated if the situation was reversed. But no one who is acceptant of other entities has ever been perfect in everything they have ever done.

Some say Jesus never sinned during his entire life in the flesh. This is a meaningless debate, for the statement is both true and false, depending on how one looks at Jesus.

Sin is a difficult concept to describe with words, but it is basically an intentional mistake which affects someone else's spirituality negatively.

Also very hard to put into words is the concept of sinlessness. From the standpoint of sinlessness being true for a person, it begins by repentance of sin and acceptance of the authority of love. When this change of heart is combined with true forgiveness by all the victims of that sinner, the result is a further cleansing of the mind and soul of that person, which is as sinless as any eternally growing entity can be.

So we could honestly say that Jesus is sinless now, for there are no longer any legitimate charges against him, which is a claim that not one of us still here in the flesh can make.

However, this is very different than saying Jesus had nothing to learn. The fact is, Jesus had a lot to learn, and always will have. Since he lives forever, he will always be growing. Do babies know how to walk immediately? Of course not, and neither do newborn spiritual babies (believers), nor does a newborn sinless child (christ). The point I am making here is that any life entity can make mistakes unintentionally, even unknowingly. This is an action that is sinless, yet incorrect, since the one who performed it is still learning. A good physical example would be a baby falling while trying to walk, or accidentally dropping something. Even adults occasionally make these errors, and the same physical principle applies to the spiritual realm.

In other words, since Jesus is growing, he will sometimes find that there was another course of action that would have been better to take on some particular matter, a course that he was unable to comprehend from the spirits that were his instructors at the time he made it. This is similar to how the spirit of Jesus spoke to Moses, but Moses was simply unable to understand all he was told. But Jesus never turned aside from the true way like we know Moses did on at least one point.

It is not just because Moses was rebuked by Jesus for his statute on divorce that makes this one law stand out. The preceding paragraphs about "mistakes" were to prepare for a discussion about an astounding revelation that the scriptures record; namely, "For your sins your mother was divorced."[1]

There are a number of meanings in this parable. One is that the mother is represented by Jacob, who symbolizes the head of the people in his day. The saying "your sins" refers to the exasperation of the spirit of Jesus with the wrongdoing of Jacob's offspring, the nation of Israel in Moses' day. But it would only be right if Jacob were divorced for his own sins. Here is a huge mistake by the spirit of Jesus.

However, we cannot discount the love that Jesus revealed to those of us who were dead in our selfishness, just because the scriptures reveal that he is growing and made many mistakes. For recall the sharp rebuke that was given to his accuser, who taunted Jesus after his resurrection for having prophesized about some of his elders in another day and age. This still dead demon insults him, saying, "Then what are these scars on your hands?" implying Jesus was rightly crucified as a criminal. But the spirit humiliates this satan with a very sharp rebuke, for Jesus answers, "I got them in my harlot's house."[2] (Many translations render the word "harlot" as "friend." Neither word quite fits, though the lesson is not completely lost with either one. The original word was closer to meaning a promiscuous acquaintance, not a prostitute, not a friend.)

This accuser he rebukes is in fact the harlot herself, still a satan, who invited him in but did not love him. Fueled by hatred, she demanded his death for his part in their mistake, though their involvement was also an error on her part. The case is plain that she was also guilty. Though Jesus did not love her like a wife, she did not love him like a husband either. And while the word "harlot" reveals and helps us understand this particular mistake the spirit of Jesus made, never forget the unsurpassed love he demonstrated as a christ, a love greater than ever before witnessed by people at our age level of spiritual understanding. True to his calling, while she and his other murderers were rejoicing over his death, he actually invoked the Eternal's blessing on them, saying, "Forgive them Father, they know not what they do."

With these words he passed judgment on himself, and the verdict was life. Jesus lives to this very day and always will.

Judas

David foresaw the spirit of Jesus cursing the spirit of Judas. He wrote of this: "It is not the taunts of a foe – that I could bear; it is not an enemy's insolence – then I could hide from him. No, you are an equal of my own, my close companion and trusted friend." Then continuing, he says, "Sweet was our fellowship together in the house of God." (This means their friendship together on earth.) "May he go to perdition. Death seize all such. May they go living to the world below, swept off as their sins deserve. For he laid hands upon his friends, profaning friendship's bonds."

Because of this and other misunderstood scriptures, most ministers preach that Judas suffered damnation. However, they are wrong, for clearly the scriptures show us that Judas is a man who found salvation.

First, the scriptures record that Judas repented. This we know must eventually bring salvation. Second, the spirit of Jesus plainly says of him, "you are an equal of my own."

This is one reason why the spirit inspires Isaiah to prophesy these profound questions: "Who is as blind as my servant, as deaf as my messenger? Who is as blind as my devotee, as blind as the Eternal's servant?"[1] These questions are not just directed to the Israelites, but are in fact parable questions asked directly of Jesus himself, and also asked of those of us who believe his message about the authority of love.

Foremost, the questions are parables to all people not ruled by love, many of whom lie to themselves by insisting that most of their problems and sufferings are caused by external forces. The truth is, except on rare occasions, a person's serious sorrows are all their own doing. And on those few occasions when they are not, they seem to forget that the spirit will more than find a way to make up for it. Furthermore, how does an occasional accidental scratch from the spirit compare to the patience of this same spirit that has endured so many of our murderous thoughts coming to life? Did we not once proclaim ourselves equal to and even above the From Everlasting? Yes, on rare occasions we are equal (behave perfectly), but we declared such wisdom our standard behavior. The tail wags the dog, we childishly insisted.

The questions are also a parable for Jesus himself, who while dying on the cross, asks, "My God, My God, why desert me? Why do my cries of anguish bring no help?" For after crying out loud with his question, he soon cries out again with the answer, this time in spirit, saying, "I am a mere worm and not a man."[2] This is a revelation for him, and for us.

Formerly, the worm is what Satan was when sin was conceived in us, but now Jesus is the worm conceiving the rejection of sin. (The "worm" is an analogy for the spiritual equivalent of physical semen in both cases.)

Now remember, the spirit plainly tells us that Jesus and Judas are equals. Does this mean that Jesus has sinned? No, but it does reveal an astounding truth that Jesus does not realize until just as he is dying – that to look at Judas is to have seen the essence of his former self – for Judas is a man exactly like himself under a different set of circumstances.

Jesus said that he picked Judas "that the scriptures might be fulfilled," but what does this really mean? For although the scriptures say that Jesus called Judas "the son of perdition," the fact of the matter is that anyone who has not repented from sin and submitted to the authority of love is a son of perdition.

And who exactly is this man named Jesus? Spiritually he was the "Son of David." David was a murderer and adulterer! No wonder Isaiah asks, "Is anyone as blind as the Eternal's servant?"

And who is as blind as David? David curses in the spirit of Jesus, saying about Judas: "May he go to perdition. Death seize all such. May he go living to the world below... For he laid hands upon his friends, profaning friendship's bonds." David never realizes (at the time) that these words of Jesus about Judas would be the very same words as Uriah's about himself![3] Talk about blind! Yet David's repentance was so great that he found forgiveness – just like Judas.

Jesus also said of Judas, "woe unto him by whom the son of man is betrayed," and again, "better for that man had he never been born."

This has to do with Judas' spiritual birth, not physical, for Jesus foresaw the impossible reconciliation Judas would have between his deed and his conscious. Some men could have ignored their guilt, kept the money, and gone on to prosper for the remainder of the age. But not Judas, he repented, and immediately at that.

And what of the last words Jesus spoke to Judas? He said, "Be quick with what you have to do." Did Judas have a choice, or was he prepared for the occasion as Jesus was?

Among the many revelations about Judas, particularly in the book of Zechariah, this one is amazing: "The hucksters who had hired me knew that this was by order of the Eternal. I said to them, If you think it right, give me my wages, but if not – never mind. So they paid out thirty pieces of silver. The Eternal said to me, Put it into the treasury, that splendid sum with which they paid you off."

Understand, I am not claiming Judas' betrayal was right, I am simply saying Judas is a man that found salvation.

David's blindness and immaturity, indeed Jesus' as well, show themselves in other ways, for remember David's curse in the spirit of Jesus that his betrayer should die and his house be left desolate. Not that such an indictment is undeserved; it is just that David, again, never seems to consider his own shortcomings – for again, these would be the very words of Uriah's against David! With those words he passed judgment on himself.

But God is slower to anger, for when David praises the Eternal, saying of God's enemies, "I hate them with a perfect hatred, I count them as enemies to myself," the spirit immediately rebukes him. The very next words David is moved to speak are these: "Search me, O God, and know my heart, test me and try my thoughts; see if I am taking a wrong course..."[4]

And the Eternal did indeed illuminate his heart, and corrected these wrong courses, and David learned to be merciful when he could. And of course, Jesus shines far beyond this, sharing with us the message that love is above all else, and demonstrating this very thing in a way almost beyond our ken, actually asking God's forgiveness of his murderers – even before he was dead by their hands. Amazing!

The scriptures record that after Jesus was arrested, "Then Judas his betrayer saw he was condemned, and repented; he brought back the thirty pieces to the high priests and elders, saying, "I did wrong in betraying innocent blood." Here we see that Judas repented, and though repentance might not stop a punishment, it absolutely must bring forgiveness in the end.

In fact, though the scriptures record the obvious hostility the other Apostles held for him, certain facts cannot be ignored, for though Judas betrayed Jesus first, it remains that all the Apostles betrayed him.

But what did Judas do? Here was a man so broken over his role in Jesus' death that he could not bear to live any longer. So he immediately killed himself that he might stand before God at once to beg for mercy and forgiveness. And this he set out to do before Jesus had even died. Such was the shame he felt at his behavior. But all the Apostles, indeed all of mankind, were guilty of letting Jesus die unjustly. For the scriptures record this prophecy: "The time to free my folk had come, I looked but there was none to help, I was amazed that there was none to aid; so my own power gained me victory."

In short, the actions of Judas were no worse than the other Apostles, for they too were guilty. We simply cannot disregard the facts that indicate some final merit on Judas' behalf. Divorced for deeds he did not commit, one might also inquire who represents Jacob in all of these things!

Indeed, though Judas betrayed Jesus first, all of the Apostles abandon him to his death – except Judas! He is the only person in the entire world defending Jesus in his darkest hour, the only one trying to stop what is about to happen. Having repented of his actions, he went back to the high priests and elders, saying, "I did wrong in betraying innocent blood," but they rejected his plea and said, "That is your affair, not ours." In fact, both Jesus and Judas hung on a tree so to speak, and both died at the same time. And while this does picture the separation of good and evil, it also symbolizes their unity, for Jesus said of Judas, through David, "you are an equal of my own."

Despite the many arguments that could be engaged in studying these facts, here is the bottom line: Judas found salvation.

As a final note, here is an answer to Isaiah's parable questions of "Who is as blind as my servant, as deaf as my messenger: Who is as blind as the Eternal's devotee, as blind as the Eternal's servant?"

The answer is that no one was as blind as Jesus. The mistakes he made that are revealed as he grows up before our eyes are proof he had much to learn. But typical of some parables, the meaning runs deep, for the reason the others questioned are not as blind as Jesus is because they see even less. The elect are blinder because of sin and the lost even more so, since their very light is darkness.

Satan

Why does the spirit of Jesus, speaking in the Old Testament, call Satan the "shining star of the dawn," but when Jesus comes in the flesh he calls himself the "bright star of the morning"?

Because the dawn always becomes morning is the answer. This is one of the things Jesus meant when he said, "If any house be divided against itself, that house cannot stand," and again, "If Satan rises against Satan, then his kingdom comes to an end." This saying from Jesus speaks of his own past.

This makes perfect sense when we think about it. We are trying to separate ourselves from the evil influences within us, and if we hold out faithfully until the end, then with the spirit's help we will have accomplished that division, thereby crossing over into eternal life. This is why Peter told us to hold on faithfully until "the day dawns, and the day star rises within your hearts."

This is delightful good news. Again, the dawn always grows into morning with its vastly greater light. Since Jesus is giving us all that is his (just as his father did for him), the only possible conclusion is that we who follow the christ Jesus are satans desiring to change our selfish ways. After all, it was on Earth that we were created, and it was to Earth that Satan fell in the beginning.

These things are in agreement with the scriptures, but far more importantly, they are also in perfect agreement with our hearts if we are honest with ourselves. The truth is that we must stand in disgrace to look back on the way we once acted and thought. Indeed, even having repented, we would be humiliated if others could hear some of the thoughts with which our hearts are so often occupied.

No wonder Jesus rebuked Peter so sharply for saying "God forbid," when Jesus told him that he (Jesus) was going to die very soon. For Peter, though he loved Jesus, was still double-minded and uncommitted to endure the cost of changing his heart, whatever form it might take, and so he hoped that Jesus might somehow fail as a christ. And what was that sharp rebuke of Jesus to his friend Peter? Namely this, "Get behind me you Satan."

Understanding what we are, and the emptiness from which we were first made, helps us better understand our life and the events within it as we grow. For all of the patriarchs and apostles held that the next life was even better, and genuinely accepted the close of their lives here, looking forward to leaving this prison and entering the true life to come.

Note that I use the word prison to make clear that this life we have now, some of it very joyful, is as angry as a loving parent gets with his wayward children.

Prophecy

The spirit of Jesus says in the Old Testament, in speaking of the coming age: "If anyone still prophecies, then the father and mother who bore him shall tell him, you must die, for in the name of the Eternal you are speaking lies."[1]

The reason why prophecy must die is because the spirit is given to all of us. Therefore we all have access to the same information. In the spiritual realm, equality of all members partaking in the spirit of love is a constant reality. So if we prophecy about another member of the spirit, in essence to declare their future to them, then we have placed ourselves above an equal. Such an attempted fortune telling, as if they were a dead object instead of another living being, is not only speaking lies, but wickedly conceited.

That kind of sinless world is what this age is supposed to try to be like, so how can we ever prophecy about our brother or sister and not incur some sort of guilt? (Note that prophecies are different than revelations, which are given to aid us occasionally.) The elect absolutely reject new prophecy and strive only to develop the fruits of the spirit that do not wear out and perish from one age to the next.

For the spiritually dead, the self-centered prophecies of a child can come to life and hold some truth of the future. However, the past few paragraphs help explain why some people rightly reject almost everything about the christ named Jesus. They had already taken "love one another" to heart, or will by some other example, so all prophecies concerning Jesus, even the true ones, are meaningless to them. Jesus understood those people who had already taken love to heart by the time he made his appearance in the flesh, and never once wickedly tried to force those childish boasts from his youth on anyone. "The old wine is good enough," is what Jesus said about the people that rightly rejected him as their lord.

Playing God

About Job and the tragedies that befell him, God said to Satan, "It was idle of you to entice me to undo him."

However, in another place, the scriptures contradict that God would ever do such a thing, for they say, "It is impossible for God to be tempted by evil." Can we resolve what looks to be God having been tempted to cruel and unjust behavior? We cannot, though we can understand what transpired.

What happened to Job, (the description that follows is not complete, but is the best I can express), is that the essence of who he once was had a conversation with the essence of who he eventually became. The talk was about himself at a stage of his growth that was after one age, but before the other, though he did not know it at any time during these phases. In short, Job past and Job future were discussing Job present. Note that all three stages are past now.

Another perspective in describing these events, seemingly different, but essentially not, (again my expression of these facts is not complete), is that the spirit of Job's bride was unknowingly having a conversation with her exact same self about him. Unlike my previous example, she is at the same level of spiritual development in both dimensions, though she does not know she is talking to herself in either dimension. Nor did she yet comprehend Job was her twin spirit and soul mate in either of these perspectives.

If we merge these two descriptions of the events we begin to form a clearer picture of what took place. We also see that a god certainly can be tempted by evil.

However, do not think it was anyone but Job and his beloved conscience who were primarily responsible for his problems. In short, the satan in him along with the god in him were both jealous and prideful over his wealth, position, and character, which provoked them to the point where they hurt themselves in an effort to be regarded as better than the other.

Happily, only love has any lasting influence, so Job and his beloved eventually emerged wiser from these accidental self-inflicted wounds.

Time Does Not Exist

Time does not exist to the sinless because they live eternally and have life inherent. Time is simply a result of sin, used as a means of measuring things by mankind. In fact, to anyone without sin, time itself can actually be molded as if it were clay, for anything without life can be molded in any way sinlessness desires.

Just as good and evil are opposite, and life and death opposite as well, so it is that eternity and time are opposite. So time is lifeless by its very nature, and as such, is utterly meaningless to the sinless.

Another way to understand that time is only real to the sinful is to realize that today is actually still the seventh day in the week of creation, the Sabbath day when God rested.

The term "day" as used in the story in the book of Genesis that describes our creation is strictly a metaphor pertaining to phases of our growth. The story is now so altered from its oral origin and retellings in the subsequent writing and rewritings that most of its meaningful information is long gone. However, it is interesting to note that Jesus said he would rebuild his temple in 3 days. Since Jesus and his bride are twins spiritually, it would be fair to conclude that she would also be using the same metaphor of 3 days. Therefore, at their rapture/reunion into one again, their new world will have been created in 6 days.

Recall what Adam and Eve were told about the tree of knowledge of good and evil: "On the day you eat from it you will surely die." This death was spiritual, not physical, for Adam and Eve lived for years after they sinned (as we think of time), and mankind itself still lives. Therefore, we can be sure that today is still that same seventh day on which God rested. In fact, it is still virtually the same instant we sinned.

It was for good reason that Jesus chose these words to question his adversaries who criticized him for working on the Sabbath: "Which of you if his sheep falls into a pit will not immediately lift it out on the Sabbath?" And, again, he said, "My father has continued working to this hour, so I work too." So we see that though God was resting he immediately came to our rescue when we fell into the pit of sin, just as any mother and father would immediately rise up to the sudden anguished cries of their child.

Different Realities

When people ask for something by which the spirit is moved, but the requests are in some way in conflict with each other, one possible result is that different realities come to exist in the same place and at the same time.

For example, two people could stand next to each other looking out over the horizon, and one of them might see pouring rain while the other sees only sunshine. If they talk about the weather, both of them will hear conversation fitting to their own perceptions. This is not some conscious or unconscious telling of lies to each other, but rather it is two souls accepting each other's right to coexistence with some heartfelt differences between them.

Different realities may also come to exist when the spirit is protecting one soul from accidentally or intentionally injuring another. And there are other reasons for such things to happen, as well. Furthermore, not only does the spirit allow such things to happen, they happen frequently, though we seldom see it.

Nevertheless, when we begin to understand the incredible power of the spirit, we realize that such things not only could happen, but that they must happen. The spirit never kills any good thing.

When God asks, "Is anything too hard for me?" and Jesus tells us "All things are possible for them that believe," then we can be sure that if the creator of heaven and earth really wants it, then the spirit will handle such a small thing as the weather. This same spirit will also act as guardian and interpreter to protect against the confusion that would result from one person's requests or hopes interfering with someone else's. However, if we want someone else's will to affect our own reality, such as a prayer for healing, then the parties involved may both see a new mutual reality.

More important are genuine thoughts of good will towards us from others, which sometimes not only affect our physical reality, but may bring us joy and even help transform our spirits. It is no small blessing when someone feels affection for us, and when others are moved to hope good things happen to us for no other reason except that they like us, we are blessed indeed.

Because of its very nature, examples of different realities in the same place at the same time are rarely recorded in the scriptures, but there are a few. For instance, at Pentecost many saw tongues of fire and heard the triumphs of God in foreign languages, but others heard only gibberish. Then at a later date, when Paul is rebuked for his persecution of believers, the spirit of Jesus appears to him in the form of a blinding light to speak to him. However, Paul's companions see nothing at all, though they hear the voice as Paul does. And Stephen saw Jesus in heaven, but his murderers saw nothing and only shrieked that he was a blasphemer as they stoned him in a jealous rage.

Yet another excellent example of different realities happening concurrently is shown by what Jesus said about the rapture of the believing. When he is asked about those people, "Where will they be taken?" Jesus replied, "Where the carcass is the vultures gather."[1] So these people stayed right where they were and simply crossed directly into the spiritual kingdom, having left the flesh behind.

Clearly then, a spiritual realm (paradise) exists right here in the same place we are, we just cannot see it very well because of our nature.

"The meek shall inherit the earth," Jesus said. And though it will not be the same world we know now, recall that it was here on earth where paradise was to begin with.

The Bride of Christ

Jesus said that John the Baptist was a better man than any other who had ever lived, while John the Baptist said of himself that he was not even fit to untie the strap on Jesus' sandal. Who then is the actual bride of the christ Jesus? And what does she look like, since scriptures record by way of parables that she is Jacob, the planet earth, and also the New Jerusalem from heaven?

The direct answer is that each of us is our own christ's bride, and vice versa. And as to the appearance of the bride, she looks the same as the groom – spiritually speaking.

Every pair of members that are joined into one physical body (arms, legs, eyes, etcetera) are always essentially identical twins. Likewise, the marriage of the christ Jesus is to an equal.

Interestingly, in paradise, the next age, heaven – whatever you prefer to call it – whenever Jesus and his bride behold each other, they appear to each other as either male or female, constantly shifting to whatever opposite gender they feel like at the moment. There is no thinking about this and it is not even noticed by them, for they do not regard it as meaningful. This happens because they share everything they are completely. Understand they are one entity, one being.

In a sense, they give control of each other to each other, subject to love, because of love.

What this means is that Jesus and his bride are to be married into one body that is equally male and female, equally give and receive. A better word for this kind of marriage is actually "reunited," but this time the union's conscience will be ruled by love instead of self.

This "one body" of equal parts give and receive is the physical example of the spiritual principle of the sinless having life inherent. And the one physical and spiritual body that they comprise is only a part of the greater spiritual body that they comprise with their father and mother, who are themselves but a part of the even greater body of the spirit itself.

They must be equally give and receive. For Jesus and his bride, while they are as one body and spirit with each other, and as one spirit with everyone else ruled by love, they nevertheless receive as much as they give. Because in their case, they give more to their children than they receive, while they receive more from their parents who are also gods than they give to them; and between themselves, the giving and receiving is equal.

Every individual sinless spiritual body has eternal life inherently and is give and receive in equal proportions.

Equality and the Sexes

Our physical bodies testify to God's desire for equality between the sexes. Just look at our own bodies to see the obvious evidence. Every pair of twin members is essentially equal: Arms, legs, eyes, ears, all basically the same, yet joined together into one body. This is a good analogy for what God wanted Adam and Eve to accomplish and is one of the reasons why he said that the two are to become "one flesh," though fulfillment of this is only possible through the spirit.

Unbelievers and spiritually immature people look at their physical uniqueness as compared to the other gender, then try to reason that they have the better temple. But this kind of attitude always proves ruinous to a marriage, since equality is absolutely required for harmony. Jesus said, "The flesh profits nothing."

Jesus also said that a husband and wife are to become "one flesh." Obviously then, the male also becomes female, and the female also becomes male. A physical example of this is plainly seen in the way every child resembles both of its parents, regardless of its gender.

If we think about the creation of Adam and Eve, the only conclusion about equality is that they were equal from the start. Different in some ways, yes, but that Eve had to have been Adam's equal becomes clear after reflecting on the matter, for there Adam stood – unhappy in Paradise!

How can that be? God was there, as was a multitude of other creatures, yet Adam was not satisfied. This is because he had no one just like himself to be with; an equal was needed. When Adam was alone in the world, his Creator had more abilities than he had, and was also capable of giving more to him than he could receive or return in response. Likewise, all of the animals had lesser abilities than Adam had, and Adam was capable of giving more to the animals than they could receive, or return to him in response. This eventually caused Adam to feel a lack of satisfaction and fulfillment. But Eve solved the problem completely. Here was a being that could receive everything he could give. And not only would that be exactly enough for her, she could return just as much as she was given.

So we see that Eve allows Adam to have a companion with equal total abilities, instead of forever being inferior or superior in total abilities to every other being. Moreover, she ended his feeling of aloneness, since she was clearly and undeniably like himself. Also, and this is very important, Eve provided Adam with a feeling of identity in the midst of infinity, a reference point, so to speak. This is very noteworthy, for "I am" may be the core of what we were given, the essence of original thought, but eventually one asks: "What am I?" and in their union Adam and Eve behold their ever-changing, never-changing answer.

About husband and wife, an enlightened scripture also says, "No man ever hated his own flesh." If we really think about this, the only conclusion is that a person's true mate is exactly what they would be if they were that sex. After all, God did exactly this for Adam, and he does not do any less for his loved ones today – if only we let him, for he is infinitely capable of finding a way to get the right two people together. In fact, most of us do marry the person God wanted us to, but our sinful natures blind us to this truth; and the curses we utter against our mate is actually testimony against ourselves.

What has Jesus told us about equality? Just the entire truth with a single question: "Can two walk together except they be agreed?" Therefore, regarding marriage, we need to understand that our closest companion and dearest friend can accept us believing that they are a little different, but never that we believe they are a little inferior.

Now if a man and a woman are supposed to join together and become "one flesh," then how much more appropriate would it be for the man and woman to join together into one spirit? The answer is, very appropriate, and this is exactly what God wanted Adam and Eve to do. After all, the Creator himself is spirit, and he is as One spirit with all the Living. Jesus himself said, "I and the Father are One." This is spiritual Oneness, not physical, and it is the same way that Jesus wants us to be with him. Jesus and the Father are not one flesh though, and neither are we with Jesus. But a man and a woman are as one flesh, so if any two should ever be as one spirit, it would have to be those who are also one flesh as well!

The point of all this is that two sinless beings who were literally perfectly matched for each other did not just look at each other, then go on their separate ways without reacting. Rather, like two magnets of opposite attractions, they saw each other and leapt for joy, immediately locking together in spiritual intercourse. We can be sure they began growing into one spiritual body composed of the two from the very moment they met; their spirits literally transforming their flesh, as he who was spiritually give and receive (and physically give), combined with her who was spiritually give and receive (and physically receive). The purpose of it all being that they should learn about love and its two directions, namely give and receive; and at the same time, to be each other's true companion – so much so that they are literally the missing part of each other!

Earlier, I noted how our individual bodies show God's desire for equality, since every pair of twin members are essentially equal. Notice also, that the single members are always at or near the center, shared by each side and linking the two halves into one complete body.

This growing together into one perfect spiritual body, with equal and perfectly matched halves sharing all the unique single members between them, was exactly the transformation that Adam and Eve's spiritual intercourse created within them. It transformed them physically, too, since sinless spiritual giving makes the flesh anything it wants, and what these two reflections of each other wanted was oneness. No doubt this new being of the two become as one spirit and one flesh, in addition to their individual identities, far surpassed their separate abilities and differed vastly from the flesh we know today.

Now at some point after Adam and Eve were completely as one with each other (probably incalculably long after they were), they wondered what would happen if they ate from the tree of knowledge (a parable), and so the temptation came to them and they eagerly accepted. The fact is, they both did exactly what they wanted, then with their new nature already in place, stood there and lied to their God by blaming their deeds on another.

The result of their sin is that they immediately began to grow apart, actually tearing apart, because their new nature was completely self-centered. Instead of sharing everything in total oneness, they now possessed the unique members individually, like before they came together without sin in the beginning. But now the flesh was deformed and defective.

What would the original sinless bodies of Adam and Eve have looked like compared to the bodies we have now? This is unknown, and unimportant, but that they were different is certain. The original bodies were created by sinless God, but the new bodies we now inhabit were the result of the one body they had become being torn in two by sin.

Imagine if your own body was waging a war for possession of your single members, the right and left halves struggling furiously for sole possession of the single central pieces like the heart, stomach, and liver, and all the other single pieces that are now shared equally. What incredible damage would be done to you as your sides tore these members away in selfishness. Imagine if the body you have now was torn in two down the middle from groin to head. What abilities would either of the two leftover pieces have compared to your whole body? This is exactly what Adam and Eve did to each other after they sinned, leaving each other with a mere shadow of the body they once shared.

As a consequence of this, the unique members were no longer shared equally in between the two of them as one body. The most noticeable of these single members are the two faces of love, give and receive, and the physical counterparts to these two members are mainly the reproductive systems. Now instead of sharing them though, their new nature of self-centeredness led them to fight to keep these single members all to themselves. When the fight to possess these members was finally over, Eve possessed the receive, and consequently Adam was left possessing the give.

Eve prevailed in this battle, not because she was formed with physical receive at creation, (remember they had become as one body and both were spiritually give first), but rather, she possessed the receive because she was slightly more selfish, since she had been corrupted by sin for a slightly longer period of time.

But this is not a thing of shame for women because Eve sinned first only because she was tempted first. This is certain, for both Adam and Eve were of the very same flesh, and both had the same sinless spirit within them. In fact, if Adam had been tempted first, then he would have sinned first and possessed the receive, consequently becoming the female as they tore apart from the oneness they had become.

But the physical damage is not the real damage, at least by comparison. The real disaster is what it represents, namely spiritual damage. This is because not only were they separated from being as one body and spirit with each other, they were also separated from being as one spirit with God and the infinite collective combined spirit, the "from everlasting to everlasting." In choosing sin they were cut off from all of this.

There was other profound damage between Adam and Eve. Now, instead of clothing one another with each other, so to speak, they were apart, and unable to rejoin because they were filled with sin, (except in a minimal physical way, which is almost nothing by comparison). No wonder they were ashamed of their nakedness. God, who moves as One, was about to behold them who had also been as one, but who were not any longer. Even worse, since they sinned, they were no longer as one with the spirit either. The multitude of catastrophic changes in their now separate bodies was shameful evidence that all had been lost in a moment.

Though we cannot be certain of the details, a mere look at our bodies indicates a host of things gone wrong. For example, men and women are generally mismatched in size and strength. How can this be? The spirit has said that a husband and wife are to be "one flesh," but the flesh is meant to be equal halves, with all the unique single members in the center to be equally shared by each half. But this physical inequality has not resulted from God's desire to shame or punish women, but rather to serve as witness that any victory in sin (fighting to possess receive) will result in a loss. However, women incur no permanent disadvantage in generally having less physical size and strength than men, since the flesh ultimately profits nothing. Furthermore, there is never any shame in it, for the spirit shows us that Eve only did what Adam would have done if he had been tempted first.

The bodies we have now bear signs of a host of other things gone astray, not least of which is that the unique single members cannot be shared (except in the most minimum way, which provides little real insight to our mate's unique perspective).

Even worse, who could fail to notice that the bodies we have now often become ill or diseased? Ultimately, they fail miserably. In other words, we die. Death is the most profound symbol of sin that we know, and that we have absolutely no hope in the flesh is understood by all.

Next, consider the incredible mind Adam and Eve had. They communicated with everyone, whatever their position, whether it was God or any of the many other creatures they shared earth with. This was done more easily than we now talk person to person. To say that we are now mentally handicapped by comparison is an incredible understatement, for the reduction in our mental faculties is like being in a coma compared to what they shared.

And what of the glorious countenance they possessed. Moses, who was a sinner like us, literally had his face aglow after talking to the lord. Adam and Eve, without sin, and who talked face to face with God every day, would have been absolutely radiant. Like pure sunlight, Adam and Eve shone quite literally like stars!

What do we have now? We perspire, urinate, and defecate. This is a long way from emitting light!

Excretions of these kinds were forbidden in the presence of the spirit of the lord under the old law, and as such, are proof that they either did not exist, or were something different than what they are now. These are just a few of the many things in our physical framework that show we are out of line with spiritual perfection, though everything that is speaks parables to us from which to learn things.

But there is one more thing that needs discussing since it is so remarkable, namely, that women menstruate. This kind of bleeding does not exist in a sinless world, since the old law declares women defiled whenever they had their periods. This is a profound symbol of two things. First, that Adam and Eve literally tore themselves apart in self-centeredness. Second, it represents sin. But not the woman's sin, it represents the children's (serpent's) sin.

This can be seen by noting the fact that most women have their periods approximately in time with the lunar cycle. But in an amazing parable, the lord pictures the man Jacob as a woman with the moon under her feet.[1] This symbolizes sin having been utterly conquered. In other words, "our enemies made a footstool for our feet," as David foresaw and recorded in the song book called Psalms. And Jacob as a woman symbolizes the unity of man and woman at the same time as sin is done away with.

All of these examples having been given, we can see clearly that today's bodies are not like the original bodies of Adam and Eve, and they are profoundly less than the glorious combined body they once shared without sin. Nevertheless, our currently damaged physical bodies still retain a symbol of give for man, and one of receive for woman, at opposite places. Why is this? Again, because give and receive are the two sides of love and completely equal in value.

Some arrogant men will be quick to twist the rebuke Jesus once gave to a woman, when he asked, "Is it not better to give than to receive?" But those who do are far astray. It was a question, not a statement of fact. The question Jesus posed was an inspired response, designed to silence the arrogance of a female who clearly hoped that being a woman was superior to being a man, but knew in her heart it was not. The truth is that one gender is as good as another.

If you doubt this, and think that give is somehow superior to receive, consider that receive is a must for fulfillment, since how could you give if no one will receive it? Furthermore, the receive must be equal to the give or dissatisfaction begins on the part of the one who is giving. Also, remember that true give, gives completely, even the ability to give is given. Anything less than that and receive begins to be dissatisfied. This unlimited giving and receiving explains how Adam and Eve could be one flesh, since their sharing was totally complete at all times, given back and forth by their spirits without sin, however their hearts desired. Knowing this is a key to understanding the parables of rejecting the equality of give and receive that are called "the worm that does not die" and "the fire that is never quenched."[2]

Love and reason both conclude that Adam and Eve, while slightly different than each other, are in no ways inferior to the other.

That "give" is explained before "receive," when a spark of love tried to explain itself to the dead, is all that was ever righteous in the old Law of Moses when talking about the gender split that resulted from our fall into sin.

Here is an analogy to explain that another way: If we are dead (standing still) and come to life (begin to move), then one day we will walk. When we try to explain what has happened, we will have to describe how one leg moved first – but both legs are equal! One leg was faithful and trusting in allowing the other to guide it for a moment, while the other was faithful and trusting in having to stand alone for a moment, keeping its word to deliver the other leg to its intended destination, which then reset itself bearing half the weight again. So we begin to walk, spiritually speaking.

Now we could continue to move in such a fashion, stopping and starting in the same order, over and over, but it soon becomes apparent that walking is much easier if we simply share the leading and following. But all of this is a simple physical example, for in the next age we will be as one with our beloved conscience, simply translating ourselves wherever our heart desires. This behavior, when joined in the spirit of love to other life entities is the beginning of our own omnipresence and omniscience.

It is important to remember that women also bear symbols of give. Breasts generally serve no purpose for a man, so does this mean that men do not give to children, or that women give more? Not at all, they only symbolize who generally goes first in giving to children. Again, this is when the spiritual tries to explain itself to the physical, manifesting examples of itself as best it can in what little remains of our former structure.

But all of these things are dead now, for the old covenant, physical in design, has been replaced by the new covenant, which is completely spiritual in design. This is proved by the spirit being given to any who will accept it, and any women in the spirit will most assuredly give first to a man still rejecting the authority of love. But then again, giving love first is not really love if it does not allow equality. True love always allows equality, regardless of who started. In fact, true love forgets who started. It simply does not care!

81

Common sense alone shows us our best friend has to be slightly different. Only you can be you. Only I can be me. The moral of all this is, stop insisting a little bit different is a little bit inferior. We cannot ever find happiness by insisting our mate is somehow inferior to our own self. Such an attitude cannot long be hidden from one's beloved, and any one of us would be inconsolably grieved to hear our very own soul mate call us a subordinate. Again, Jesus has revealed the entire truth with a single question: "Can two walk together unless they be agreed?" Surely this makes sense. If the two are to be as "one flesh," how will it be if one half is inferior? Picture an entire body with one arm shorter, one eye dimmer, one ear deafer – what a hardship that would be. If one leg is shorter than the other, how will they walk together in agreement?

Now I ask another question – answer it honestly: Who among us has not wondered what it would be like to be the opposite sex? Not like some of the young take to heart, but rather in a way led by the spirit, so we could really know what each other's unique differences are like? That would be great. What a terrific gift, to let your companion experience your unique temple. (More accurately, I could say "experience the other side of their temple.") Still, there exists an even better gift, the actual sharing of each other's minds. Wow! These are amazing things, yet none are as great as the best gift of all, the one that was given to us all, for all of these things are the result of us having been given love, the power and gift of life itself.

Lastly, look at some truly profound scriptures, things that are difficult to comprehend mentally and harder to explain with words. First, what does the spirit mean when it says, "Ask now and inquire, if ever a man is with child...what day is like it? An hour of travail for Jacob; but he shall come through it."[3] A true prophecy also foretells that "frail woman becomes manly." Even more amazing is the revelation vision that a christ gave to the Apostle John, showing Jacob as a woman giving birth to a christ.

There are a lot of meanings in these parables, but I am moved to let the reader solve these cornerstone things on their own. However, I will note that Jesus called mankind the "sons of women," but called himself the "son of man."

Jesus said that we should treat others the way we would want to be treated, and he also said that however we judged others, the same method would be used to judge us. This being the truth, it would be wise to treat and judge our very own mate as an equal. Refusing equality always prevents a union from finding true happiness, the result being walking together limping, or even worse, walking alone.

One final question to the satan in all of us: If we are not willing to be an equal with our very own perfectly matched companion, then who would we ever be willing to call an equal?

Inexorable Conclusions

Fill in the blanks: one, two, three, four, five, six, seven, _____, _____, _____. I believe the next numbers are eight, nine, and ten. What do you think?

In the same way, the mature believer develops a clear understanding of spiritual things that are not written in the scriptures. But we can know them, even if we have not actually seen or heard them before.

In fact, there comes a time for the spiritually mature when limiting discussion of spiritual things to only the scriptures is not only tiresome and remedial, but absurd.

Understanding even progresses to an advanced point where spiritual things become so deep and personal that discussing them aloud seldom happens at all. Instead, most discussions of spiritual matters quietly take place between our conscience soul and the spirit within us. And as we become advanced in our understanding, we discard the immaturity and serious fallibility of written guidance, entrusting our souls to the vastly superior authority of the spirit of love within us.

This means that both the scriptures and church attendance become remedial as we grow in the spirit of love. This is much the same as children progress to calculating higher math and leave behind the discussion of the ten basic numbers they once studied in depth. Imagine mathematicians forced to study the addition or multiplication tables their entire lives. It would be ridiculous. Yet for children, basic math is a challenge and delight to master. The same can be true for studying the scriptures, at least the enlightened bits and pieces they contain. But the serious student of life will find that the spirit of love, and God's creation itself, hold so much more spiritual enlightenment as to render any religion and its scriptures virtually useless by comparison.

Remember what Jesus said to the Apostles: "I have many more things to tell you, but you cannot bear them at present. But when the helper comes, he will reveal all things."[1] So we see that there are many more things to be revealed to us which were never spoken of by Jesus.

In fact, spiritual maturity does not require any study of the scriptures whatsoever, or any kind of church going. Suffice to say, only love, which brings with it the fruits of the spirit, is necessary for growth.

In short, any religion and its scriptures are of little value to the vast majority of people, and of no long term value to anyone. However, no one who is advanced in their understanding who would ever curse the christ Jesus, (not even those elders who rejected him, of whom Jesus approved, saying of their reasoning, "the old wine is good enough"). In short, only a demon would curse someone for repenting of selfishness and deciding to love others.

So study whatever scriptures you want. Attend a church if you want. An open heart and mind will usually gain a little from listening to someone else's interpretation of God. But expect to outgrow such things if you are really seeking answers to life's questions. We were made by our god, and in our god's image, and dwell in a world created by his power. Therefore, all of the answers to life's questions are automatically to be found within us, and around us.

Churches and scriptures are all man-made, so even if they avoid the crime of telling us how and what to think, they are still other people suggesting those things. What we are, by definition, must outgrow such tutoring and find us thinking for ourselves. Not only would such a proxy be bad for spiritual adults, it is not even permitted, for to presume authority to think for a peer is as wicked as any conceit ever known. We have all been given the vastly superior spirit of love that lives within us, and this is the only true word of god for each of us.

The physical representation of god can be seen in the world on which we dwell. It is also seen in a limited way in our individual bodies, in which our own spirits dwell. Along with our own spirit, the spirit of god can also dwell within us. This is a fact, for having been made in god's image, the spirit automatically shares everything good that we are able to receive. Mere common sense reasoning about the nature of god confirms this must be so, yet even without reasoning, we somehow innately know that we can share this spirit and have access to its tutelage whenever we want. In short, every one of us can communicate directly with the spirit of god, which communicates back to us on the highest level each of us is able to comprehend, always doing so guided by its endless love.

Paul once rebuked a church that was interested in keeping the old physical laws, asking: "Did you begin with the spirit, only to end with the flesh? Are you such fools?" This is terrific logic, but Paul did not see how far it goes.

Not only does Paul's excellent question also apply to us about his own interpretation and subsequent teachings about "what god says," it even applies to a man as inspired as Jesus, who was also flesh. We must follow the spirit of love. Jesus rightly rejected being called "good" by an admirer, for Jesus replied to him, "Only God is good."

We begin life with the eternal, invisible word of god speaking within us, surrounded by a temporary visible word of god around us. Can anything spoken by any person replace that authority? Are we such fools?

Commentaries and Encouragement

The Power of Thought

Imagine going someplace by simply wanting to be there. What would it be like to do something simply by saying it will be done? These are amazing concepts to contemplate, and though far beyond our abilities, we somehow glimpse that such ideas will one day be a reality for us. Even our dreams hint at such things.

How fast is the speed of thought? This is not a question with a definitive answer, but we can conceive an idea of the speed of thought by understanding that the speed of light would sometimes be standing still by comparison. Even more astounding is that the speed of thought is the slowest a god works, not the fastest.

This is because a god (one without sin), in whom no darkness dwells, often moves at the speed of instinct or reflex. In other words, love instantly does the right thing, sometimes without even thinking. For just as we sinners are quick to think evil thoughts, but the impulse in our hearts to sin is often faster, so it is in an opposite way that a god's thoughts can be quick to think and then do what is good, but the impulse of such a heart often moves even faster. In short, a god can communicate the essence of what they are trying to say or do instantaneously.

It is difficult to comprehend what it would be like to have this kind of mind. No person in the same spiritual age as we are can understand it very well. But if we always fight taking sinful thoughts to heart, then pure instincts and reflexes must slowly develop within us. This is exactly the same principle of how a repetitive exercise always builds muscle.

As we understand time, if I said a million years, this might be just a fraction of the time for us to get to such a place of instinctual goodness. But what is that compared to eternity? It is not even a moment compared to the Eternal, the "from Everlasting." This helps us understand how any of the infinite number of sinless gods declare of themselves, "I Am" and can do any good thing they want by simply declaring, "It Is."

Nothing Is Hidden

The spirit hears our lies and genuinely hateful words, even when we are not talking. The same is true, or course, for genuinely loving thoughts. It is not our voices, but rather the sincere heartfelt meanings of our words and thoughts that the spirit understands. Put simply, if we were thinking it from the heart, we said it, and members of the spirit heard every word.

Jesus understood the importance of proper thinking. He knew that when he was thinking, his thoughts were not just things he had already learned that had become a part of his own conscious being, but that the thoughts could also be words from his lord, his father, or any member of the spirit. Thoughts can also be from lawless spirits (demons), which are simply those spirits who have not yet accepted the authority of love. Foremost of these demons is each person's own satan.

There are many things to say about thinking, about what it is and what it can do. But I want to focus on one particular aspect here, specifically, the incredible unity of the "Spirit" that contains an infinite number of members, who collectively say of themselves, when speaking to the dead, "I am One God", and, "There is no other God but me." How can such unity and oneness exist?

The answer is that all members accept each other as equal in value, never sin, and let love be their guide as the rightful highest authority. And one of the things that the sinless can share is each other's thoughts and feelings.

When this happens, then to think something from the heart is to have spoken it, to desire something is to have it. If the desire involves other members of the spirit, it does require their accord, however. That is the world we are becoming a part of, where thought and reality are often the same. So what will happen to us in the next world, where there is no flesh and only our spirits dwell? We can see the potential problem, which is why Jesus told us to try to get our thoughts in check, as well as our deeds. For example, he warned us that "to look upon another with lust is to have committed adultery in our hearts."

Recall what happened to Isaiah, a sinner like us. Taken in the spirit to appear before the lord and a host of other spirits, the first words out of his mouth were, "Woe is me, I am a dead man, for I am a man of unclean lips."

No wonder he was in terror for his life. While he could hear glorious thoughts and feelings of love that are impossible to describe, they in turn could hear and feel the corruption and weakness in every thought he had – and he knew it. Just picture the scene: A fair comparison of Isaiah's feeling about himself as he stands in the midst of this harmonious group is that he knows he is a dog by comparison.

Ask yourself, how would you fit into a society like heaven? Think of your every heartfelt thought being broadcast over a public loudspeaker, then ask yourself, are you really ready to talk with the sinless face to face?

But take heart, we will be ready when the time comes if we are obedient to the authority of love, for it cleanses us in preparation to enter the next age, just as it did those who entered life before us. With love, we can go without fear. Our spiritual parents do not expect us to be without need of care. They will rejoice at our arrival, just the same as physical parents rejoice over the birth of a long awaited infant. And this time when we are born into a new world, instead of awakening with crying, like we did entering this life, we awaken with a joy as great as laughter!

Under Construction

Everyone in our age is under construction, literally in the spiritual womb, so to speak, hopefully growing day by day, moment by moment.

Just as mother's milk is the first thing we receive to sustain our physical life, so it is that the air itself contains the first thing we receive that sustains our spiritual life. We all begin receiving physical sustenance soon after we are born, or we die. But much more important is the spiritual, contained in the invisible air we breathe. It is literally the first thing we do, or we will not live at all. And the very last thing we do at leaving this life is exhale.

Inside milk is a wide variety of nutritional elements that help us to grow, but the majority of this food is eventually determined to be of no benefit and is therefore eliminated from the body as waste, returning to the earth from whence it sprung.

The same principle applies to the spiritual and therefore our thought processes. In the air is contained every invisible thought or combination of thoughts that has ever been generated by living entities (but never every thought or combination of thoughts that ever will be). Whether it is spiritual, mental, or emotional, or some combination of these seemingly distinct but inseparable elements, we may intake a particular thought or combination of thoughts, like them, and so give them a home. But those that we reject are discarded and return to the spirit that generated them, or in the case of lawless spirits, to the darkness they have been semi-abandoned to, the experience being some amount of good, bad, or indifferent for all involved.

This is similar to the way we create a thing physically, but may then realize we no longer need it, of find some error or insufficiency in it. In the case of error or deficiency our solution is always to see if we can modify it, but if that fails then our created thought may get discarded. However, higher levels of spiritual awareness, which we seek, but have not yet attained, never completely discard what they create. Love always allows a thing to correct itself, even isolating the thing if need be for the protection of others.

Each of us are a thing similar to that, a vast conglomerate of thoughts in one being is what we are. And all of us are, or were isolated, needing or formerly needing to accept the authority of love. If we accept this minor change we will not be rejected as waste, instead finding we automatically now belong as a member of the spirit.

There is real peace of mind, even joy, in having a "live and let live" attitude that comes from love. By accepting the rights of others "to be," we find ourselves granted the same fairness and are much better able to pursue whatever our own hearts desire. This is not only because having allowed others this basic right elevates our mind and soul to another level, but also because this attitude finds others more willing to assist us when they are able.

Demons

At the very instant we take an evil thought to heart a demon will enter our body. Even if the thought was simply to deny something that we know to be true (which is of itself an evil thought), a demon will enter. This always happens, without fail, regardless of how minuscule the error might have been. Such events are always accompanied by a twinge of pain to some degree, though usually so faint that we just ignore it, or do not even notice. Naturally, correct thoughts cause no discomfort at all, often even bringing noticeable comfort with them.

Learning to think is just a part of growing spiritually, so such mistaken thoughts are not a big problem, unless the errant thought taken to heart is being nurtured by its host. Moreover, the errant thought does not usually need immediate attention unless its host is considering giving it life by acting upon it in some way.

The reason the spirit is not concerned about straining out tiny specks is because the little demons will get swept away with larger ones when they are cast out. Any genuine thought of love that finds its way into actuality expels a multitude of wrongly harbored thoughts from our hearts. However, many demons can rush back in like the tide of the sea returning, if the person performing the work is prideful about it. In fact, the power of love is so great that even simple gratitude by recipients of a good deed can cause a multitude of demons to flee from them.

On the other hand, whenever we reject an evil thought without taking it to heart, the demon is rebuffed and returns to the darkness without entering us.

But what if the demon (evil thought) we now reject is one which we had formerly taken to heart? In the case of corrected thoughts, the demon is rebuked and immediately flees from the body to return to darkness, sometimes slightly wiser for having lived next to a greater light than itself. Interestingly, cast-out demons almost never flee our bodies from whatever particular place they entered us. This has do with them concealing their true nature from the other thoughts dwelling within us from the very beginning they take residence.

94

Lastly, a demon that is cast out never causes any pain when it goes, only relief to the extent it was a burden.

Illness and Injury

It is unpleasant to think about why do people get sick or injured, but it does happen frequently and the reasons why it does should be considered.

There are a number of reasons why illness or injury might occur, but three in particular come to mind.

The first reason is that the spirit is punishing us for sin or mistreatment against another life entity.

The second reason is that it was a chance happenstance and is being allowed to take place. Under this heading might fall the problems resulting from inexperience, ignorance, accident, and similar types of things. Even curiosity can often be blameless. The spirit never allows harm to be the final result of these kinds of chances to those that are elect, even if the end result is death. The spirit always uses these random situations in some way to witness the nature of love.

The third reason is that illness or injury is caused by interceding for another life entity, or on behalf of the principle of love of itself.

The first reason signals that we are doing or have done something wrong. The second represents neither right nor wrong, only that the spirit is allowing a random chance to stand for some purpose. And the third signals that we are doing, or have done something right. Whatever the cause, it is up to us to talk it over with our god to discover the reason, or combination of reasons for the problem.

If it is a friend who is ill or injured, we do not want to be like Job's comforters were. Blind to mercy and compassion, they questioned his righteousness and passed judgment on him without pity. And though Job's trials and tribulations stemmed in part from his pride, remember, the spirit has testified that Job was as righteous a man as any in the land. If such things can happen to him, they can happen to any of us.

Instead, if we really love our friends, we will ask the spirit to have mercy, and to give them understanding and to heal them.

Lastly, it is important to note that illness and injury are not, and never have been, primarily due to luck or fate, two popular explanations to thoughtlessly describe what no one wants to spend much time really thinking about. Luck or fate, if viewed incorrectly, lead to critical mistakes, since they imply that the spirit of God is arbitrary or capricious, even unmerciful.

Luck is just another word for chance, but it has no ability to stop or slow illness and injury like interceding for another can. Likewise, luck has no ability to originate or speed illness and injury like intentional wrongdoing. When chance illness or injury is allowed to happen by the spirit, one of the other two reasons is often involved. Stop and think: Does mere chance have the same authority as love? Of course not, so we can take heart and live without fear, for the effect of chance on the elect is almost non-existent compared to those ruled by self.

As to fate, meaning a thing "had to happen," this is false when it comes to unhappy things like illness and injury. To try to direct the fate of another living entity in matters dealing with pain, suffering, or death is never for any adult to play with. Children though, do experiment with playing almighty god in their immature self-centered fantasy universes. On the other hand, determining that it will be fate for a good thing to happen is the occasional work of adult behavior. It is always lawful to do good.

Whatever happens to us, happens with our god's knowledge. Remember, Jesus said, "Are not two sparrows sold for pennies? Yet not one of them will fall to the ground unless your father wills it." So we do not want to be like those who attribute sorrowful things like illness and injury to luck or fate. Such a conclusion is hoping to be excused from the responsibility of our actions, or disregarding our god's knowledge of the events in cases of random chance allowed to stand.

At the end of this life, when we pass on to the next age after "dying" from something, there is no need to fear. Just as a pregnant woman is anxious at the time of delivery, and the event itself is usually accompanied by pain, she immediately forgets all of that as she rejoices over the baby. So it is that when we pass through to the next age, all of this "dying" will be utterly forgotten in our infinite joy on arrival.

Multitudes

Considering that Jesus compared the death of one of the elect and sleeping to be the same thing, it prompts this question: Where do we go when we are sleeping? Assuming we are among the elect, would it not be the same place as when we die?

Our entire body, as we know it, is a living parable. Consider that Satan took one third of the angels when he fell. Look how this relates to our bodies in that we generally sleep about one third of each day. In addition, this perfectly fits the companion parable of 666 being called the number of Satan's name. This 666 represents two thirds, and of course, this is the approximate amount of time each of us spends awake each day. Add the fractions together and the result is one.

Whether awake or sleeping, both conditions serve good purpose, for the essence of who and what we are remains basically the same in either dimension. That being the case, the spirit sometimes uses one dimension to help the other. Have you ever met yourself in your waking hours? You surely have, and in your dreams you have met yourself, too. Interacting with another individual, only to realize later that the person was the exact essence of ourselves is not always a pleasant experience either, for seeing ourselves as we really are is often depressing. No wonder one scripture laments, "The heart is desperately wicked, who can understand it?"

Nevertheless, the blessing of those ruled by love to be "scattered like dust" is more than just infinite offspring. It is also the fulfillment of dreams, all the things we hope. This happens by sharing the very essences of ourselves with those we love, and in so doing, each of us will eventually become a kind of individual multitude. We are one, each of us an individual living entity, yet we are also becoming infinite, part of everything.

As much as the oak is greater than the acorn, indeed as much as a planet is compared to a grain of sand, so is our future compared to the present. In fact, through the power of love, we will all become entire universes, one of and part of the infinite.

Spiritual Evolution

Bible literalists insist that man did not evolve from apes, but the evidence of some kind of kinship in the geological record is overwhelming to anyone who looks honestly. Personally, I think a simple visit to the zoo is all the proof needed.

This is not to say creation does not exist. Things have an origin, and I believe creation explains the missing links in the geological record of the progression of all species. Without sin and all the problems contained within it, including the memory of having done intentional wrong, an entity can change simply by wanting to, instantly. The point is, not only is there original creation, but creations keep happening, just as evolutions do.

The difference between the two is that creations are generated more by the will of spirit, while evolutions are more the result of physical forces. This is generally speaking and overly simplified, for both go together in small to large part, depending on what is needed or wanted, plus other variables.

The evolution of mankind shows us growth and change, physically and spiritually. On an individual level, our lifetime is a physical and spiritual evolution. And during this period, another kind of growth and change is happening, a kind of social evolution, as we grow to take a place in society. We attempt to harmonize our individual physical and spiritual presence with others, and find ourselves generally forced to be less self-centered and more accepting of the rights of others. Various societies and the rules we invent for them are a result of this.

However, in the purely spiritual realm, no set rules are ever needed for interaction between multiple entities, for everyone is partaking in the same spirit of "love one another." This is something many churches and all religions have trouble with, for no hierarchy can exist when love is everyone's authority. Indeed, many individuals have great difficulty accepting this, and many false leaders have been exposed when they can no longer conceal that they hate equality with those they are supposed to be helping.

This is not to say that the right institutions, run properly, never make it a little easier for an individual person to love. But history shows organized religions have done profoundly more harm than good. This is because the people that maneuver to run these institutions are usually not truly ruled by the authority of love. As ministers, they are far more politician than teacher, blindly refusing to accept that they have absolutely no authority to dictate to anyone what to think, what to believe, what to say, or what to do, since the spirit of love is given to us all.

Yet the pharisees insist that we follow their individual or group interpretation of what to think and do about this love, instead or our own god-given understanding. How arrogant does a person have to be to pretend to know someone else's identity and infinity better than that individual?

Look where organized religion has taken us, and I will cite but a fraction of the crimes:

In the name of God, the leaders of the Mosaic religion, now known as Judaism, commanded the people to slaughter entire nations, even the babies. Prior to this, we are told their god executed every first born child of an entire nation. What ego, blindness near to insanity. They even had a death penalty for anyone who insulted their god.

Not to be outdone, when the Christian leaders came to have power they plundered the entire world "in Jesus' name." For centuries they enslaved entire nations, repressed freedom of thought, and all the while were banishing or executing every effective dissenting opinion. And by what authority? More madmen who truly believed God held them superior to all others.

In Islam we see the same crazy leadership. Their societies today are reminiscent of years ago in the other religions I cited. The women have virtually no rights and the people are indoctrinated to oppose other points of view as evil. This behavior does not sound like the results of any good thing one might learn from reading the Koran. Where is the respect for the different beliefs of other people? But this is only temporary, indicative of the level of Islamic evolution.

Even with Islam's present lunacy wherein some Muslims are committing random murders as love offerings to their still dawning god, the other religions cannot brag a whit more wisdom. This is because of Judaism's and Christianity's earlier heinous crimes, the weight of which still lingers.

All of these religions ultimately fail miserably for the spiritually mature, since true love always grows to see any system of religion as the falsehood it is.

Even the very best of individual churches become remedial for the spiritually mature. Physical parents try hard to raise children who can one day leave the nest and support themselves. The same principle applies overwhelmingly in the spiritual sense. But organized religions and most churches do not seek such a godly goal. Their reasons are obvious and ugly, and in so doing they reveal the awful true nature of those kind of leaders. And the fact that all of these so-called great religions still do not acknowledge the only real authority is love proves the general absurdity of them all.

Not only is it the right of every individual to interact in all spiritual matters directly with their own god and soul, it is required from any adult.

Love simply cannot be an organization of any kind, whether religious, political, business, or social. It is a way of life, which is the end of self-centeredness. By definition it allows equality and negates the rights of any group to dictate beliefs to another group, and negates the right of any person to dictate beliefs to another individual.

More importantly, love negates the right of any group to dictate beliefs to any individual, even a group without sin. Which is how new life, something from nothing, a satan, can arise.

Just as important, as concerns the subject of this book, love negates the right of any individual to dictate beliefs to the group. Once any satan accepts this (for they certainly understand it), the dawn passes into the sunrise of a christ, which then seeks to repair the selfish damage it once had a hand in.

Of course, this wickedness of organized religions does not mean that no good has ever been accomplished by them, for love is never wasted, and we do see them growing. However, the fact remains that only love is in authority, and again, while an occasional church may be beneficial to a community, by definition, an organized religion becomes incapable of doing more overall good than harm.

We are all individuals, and every one of us will interpret the exact same thing differently, in very minute to very large degree. Love is too big to be fully contained in any thing or any person that ever has or ever will exist, including Jesus, Moses, Mohammed, Buddha, Gandhi, you or me, or any person – past, present, or future. Though love can be within us, and we can seek to make it a permanent part of ourselves, as demonstrated by people throughout the ages.

Rituals and Traditions

There is nothing inherently bad about rituals and traditions, but nothing necessarily good either, so common sense dictates we need freedom to examine routines.

For example, do we still need circumcision? This ritual was symbolic of a man giving his manhood to his wife and becoming a female in return. In the spiritual sense, it represents the two (give and receive) become as one eternal living entity of equal parts give and receive.

The sentiments this ritual represented are truly noteworthy. It stands as a stunning testament to how amazingly far our hearts were able to see with the tiniest spark of love. However, the old law's physical covenants have all expired, having been replaced by the spiritual covenant of love.

Other rituals are just plain sanctimonious, for example, when the practitioners of priestcraft tell us to get on our knees and talk to God publicly. Talking to God, and praying, which is more of an entreaty to a higher power than conversation, are things of a generally private nature, and rarely is it appropriate to do either on our knees. It may look reverent, but honest reflection on the matter results in our being offended, for it exists only to make us more subjective to the will of those who tell us to kneel. Which of us would demand their children approach on their knees to speak to us? If we, with all our faults, heartily embrace talking with our children face to face, then how much more so our heavenly parents!

The list of meaningless, even wrong, rituals and traditions is long in every day and age, for every people and nation. One current obscenity in my homeland consists of millions of little school children taking oaths to our flag, in essence training them to blindly follow the policies of our nation, as if our leaders never make mistakes. The sole purpose of this ritual is to brainwash future adults to be obedient to the status quo, subordinating, even disowning their own points of view, which are often better than our national policies. Children should be taught they are a citizen of the world, moreover, one day a citizen of the infinite, instead of instilling them with myopic nationalist pride.

Some organized religions want public prayers in these same schools for these impressionable young minds. This is a useless activity, ignored by the spirit for the pharisee behavior it is. The true goal of such things is brainwashing, exactly the same as flag worship, if I may express it as such.

It is mental rape, a harsh description that is perfectly fair given the age of the recipients, to imprint defenseless little children with any political, philosophical or religious doctrines, except the principles contained in "love one another," which are universal constants.

I am sure you can think of some other senseless standards yourself, so I will not labor over further examples.

The point is that we should question and examine anything which our hearts lead us to have an honest look at, no matter how established the behavior, and then discard those customs that we discover are wrong or that we have outgrown.

Predestination and Free Will

Mankind is subject to predestination and free will, rather than one or the other. They work together, and among other things, are like levels of awareness.

One way to help visualize this is to pair either of these concepts with the physical or spiritual realm. This simplistic approach results in four combinations: predestination and physical, free will and physical, predestination and spiritual, free will and spiritual.

The first combination would be predestination in the physical realm. This one is mere machinery. The plant world is much like this.

The second possibility is free will in the physical realm. Here we have the animal world, including people, each of us dwelling in the organic machinery we call our bodies. The first combination of predestination in the physical realm is still the primary force operating in the animal world, for our bodies grow and then decline automatically. But in obeying the inherent needs and urges these bodies generate, we have something new here, for many animals, in varying degrees, are able to use free will in directing their actions to best satisfy themselves, both physically and spiritually (which includes emotionally).

The third pairing would be predestination and the spiritual realm.

When free will in the physical realm acts truly unselfishly, such behavior, even if miniscule, is an act of love. And the predestination that happens here, in the spiritual sense, is that the spirit of love, which is an eternal flame, so to speak, recognizes itself in that spark of new love and will forever shepherd this new life until that entity is self-sustaining, meaning totally committed to the authority of love. From a standpoint of predestination, it is important to note that this is more like assistance or guidance by the spirit than it is control. The spark has free will to respond to the impetuses as it wishes.

Of course, the fourth combination is free will in the spiritual realm. Here is the place where love, and therefore life, is eternal. This is the highest level that exists. When entities having life inherent interact, free will is always the rule between them, never predestination.

These are simple descriptions, and it is very important to note that in the truest sense, these things are not divided, but rather all combined into one. However, love always has the highest authority.

In the course of this book I touched upon the subject of our thoughts sometimes coming to life, often without our realizing it. I also talked about different realities in the same place and time. Let me add that a large part of everyone's entire life, (spiritually speaking) is literally custom made for us. This predestination, as it is, continues through our lives, though less spiritual lessons are pre-planned for us as we mature and begin to embrace the authority of love. This goes together with the fact that the more we embrace that authority, the more say we have in matters concerning our spiritual selves.

A physical example of this would be how a child's day could be largely planned. The parents know almost everything that will happen to the child that day, since they were the cause, having pre-planned the day's events. Yet, for the child, everything that happened was seemingly random or spontaneous. These childhood days when nearly everything was completely planned for us pass in just a few years into adulthood and almost all free will.

But in the spiritual sense, pre-planning by a higher authority operates during our entire life. It does decrease, but it never stops. Our spiritual parents never stop tending to us at this age. After all, even the physically eldest of us are mere babies spiritually. However, as always, we have the free will to interact and respond to the spirit as we please.

In short, predestination is a primary essence of the physical realm, while free will is a primary essence of the spiritual realm.

Miracles

Personally, I have witnessed several events that I could only describe as miracles, and I know a multitude of other people have their own amazing stories they could tell.

Events like these, when private or personal, surely contain some blessing. But fanfare displays of miracles are another matter, always false to those already ruled by love.

All talk of the fictional stories about Jesus aside, when he says we should "love one another," our hearts tell us this is pure truth, for the meaning of words like that carry with them their own authority.

To say it plainly, almost all of the miraculous stories throughout the Bible are pure fiction. Did Jesus feed a multitude with a few fishes and loaves? No. Though by moving the hearts of those who attended that sermon, so many had a change of heart and decided to share what they had hidden away, that all ate heartily. This is a spiritual miracle.

Did Jesus raise Lazarus from the dead? Physically speaking, the answer is no. Spiritually speaking, the answer is yes, for Lazarus submitted to the authority of love, and for this reason Jesus did say about Lazarus' death that he was only sleeping.

Did Jesus cure blind and deaf people? Physically speaking, the answer is essentially no, for each of us must be willing to do the work ourselves. Spiritually speaking, the answer is yes, for he was the inspiration for many. The ministry of Jesus was spiritual, not physical in design. When he said "the blind see" and "the deaf hear" he was talking spiritually.

The tampering with the original facts about Jesus' ministry and the overwhelming amount of fanciful additions to these human interpretations by businessmen is staggering. Within the first 100 years after Jesus' death they had turned him into a sort of magical wizard. However, calm and logical reflection makes it clear that no miracles are necessary for us to believe Jesus' message about the authority of love. In fact, miracles would only cheapen his message. The greatest thing we will ever know is love. It stands on its own and requires no showmanship for this to be understood. The extremely few miraculous healings Jesus ever bestowed or inspired happened privately, so only the effected person was actual witness to the changes.

Jesus knew love was the key to eternal life! This is the real miracle he was trying to share with us dead souls! His selfish and childish days of self-aggrandizing boasts and lording dominion over his realm were long gone. Jesus came to us offering and accepting equality with anyone who was willing.

Nothing supernatural is necessary for us to recognize the ultimate authority of love he preached, and no divinity on the part of anyone who says love is the only true authority is required to make it be understood either. We either accept it, or intentionally stay in the dark. Inherently, we recognize the sentiments contained in love as perfectly right for our spiritual life, just as we understand our need to breathe air for our physical life. The meanings contained in sayings like "love one another" are the wisest possible thoughts that will ever exist.

Try to picture, against the backdrop of eternity, the effect this thought of the ultimate power of love has as it takes hold in any satan's heart, the dawn of real creation. Unable to deny love's authority any longer, a light starts to shine in the awakening creature.

And in what way does love manifest itself at the very beginning? The answer is that this light of love manifests itself almost entirely self-centered, as opposed to the creature being totally self-centered which it was but a moment before. This helps explain some of the childishness of the infant spirit of Jesus in the Old Testament, or the selfish childishness of all people.

"Love one another." Perfection is contained in the meanings of this saying, and we all know it immediately, though in our self-centeredness we all hesitate to take it to heart.

Christ

Compared to what we must endure, was it easier for Jesus to understand things, since he was able to talk to God directly, whenever he wanted?

Are we not in the same position, able to talk with God directly and whenever we want? Of course we are, and the truth be told, we always were, until the businessmen took control of the stories about Jesus, exaggerating his person while discounting the rest of us.

This exaggeration about Jesus was easy to do, since his learning was so enlightened compared to many of his peers. Some of the people were so jealous or misunderstanding of his teachings that he wound up being accidentally and intentionally killed.

"No greater love exists than that a person lay down his life for his friends." This is an exact truth spoken by Jesus. Yet multitudes of other people have done this very thing, both before and after his ministry. By Jesus' own words, all such people are equal to him.

Furthermore, to clarify, dying for your friends is not the only greatest love, for love is not divided. Not all are called to serve in the same way, and those to whom more is given, more is required. However, all of us do have to be faithful to the authority of love, no matter what the consequences!

So what does it mean to be a christ? One way to answer is to say it is the period of life between discovering love and then finally submitting to the authority of it. Or, one could say it is a phase in life, very much like the pupa stage between being a caterpillar and then a butterfly. Other analogies to describe what takes place is that it is like the bridge crossing from being false to choosing to be true, or the bridge from dead to alive. The best analogy may be that it is simply self-centered choosing to be all-centered.

Astoundingly, this whole phase happens without that individual christ quite realizing it, very much like a dream. But it does not happen without witnesses, for the dead that awake to the spark of love that any christ represents will credit the source. And every one of us who chooses to be ruled by love becomes a shining light of life for an additional multitude of demons.

But the fact is that Jesus is not the spark for everyone, indeed he is not the spark for most. For the vast majority of people it will be someone else who changes their hearts, and there is a never ending multitude of others that will follow them.

As for myself, I will always credit my wife as the spark of love most responsible for awakening my soul and saving me from the second death. She is my christ and I will love her forever, first and foremost of my friends.

God is Love

The words God and Love are often used interchangeably, since they are in many ways essentially the same thing. However, ultimately there is no such thing as "God," for we are all gods, and spiritually live in a world where all life that is ruled by love is equal in value, even if not in ability. To be exact, this thing called love is a concept, the highest ideal, and is never an individual life form.

The problem with trying to convey this concept from person to person is that words must fail to completely describe the power of love, just as any other device must fall short in conveying the essence of what ultimately contains everything.

In the Christian scriptures the word God is used in many places. Often, it means no more than the spirit of Jesus, particularly in the Old Testament. Sometimes it means the collective spirit, that is to say Jesus and the infinite number of other life entities ruled by the authority of love. This meaning is more common in the New Testament.

The word "god" as we presently use it has many definitions, and these various interpretations of the word can be useful for the purpose of teaching or communicating ideas. Sometimes the term is used to label an entity which came before us, or one with more love, or more wisdom, or more power, and sometimes the term simply describes who brought us into being – our author, as it were. However, ultimately there is no such thing as "God," for only Love is to be revered above all else.

At one point in my lifetime I saw everything more clearly than my son. Stated plainly, when he was a baby I was essentially god to him. But he also has the spirit within him, and as the years have passed and he has grown from childhood to manhood, he has often added to, and occasionally even corrected my thinking on one subject or another. The latter does not happen frequently, but it is happening more and more often as he matures. Since we will both be growing forever, in the spiritual sense, he may never pass my total level of understanding, but he surely will equal it, for the gap is closing. I like that. In fact, he is welcome to know all that I understand. It is my pleasure to share and it is my delight to learn from him, as well.

The same spiritual principle applies: If we, with all our human frailties, delight in our children maturing to where we increasingly communicate with them as brothers and sisters (and this happens in just a few years), then how much more so do our heavenly parents extend equality to us over the span of forever!

There is no one person who is God above all others. God is love.

Deism

Any person who honestly uses their power of reasoning must conclude there is a higher power than mankind. The proof of this is self-evident in the creation itself. True religion is a personal matter between man and his maker by its very nature, and can never to be dictated by one person to another. Furthermore, anything from man that professes to be "the word of God" is inherently false.

That is a basic overview of general deist philosophy today. It mirrors my beliefs in many ways, and I have left all of organized religion and their man made words of God behind.

However, I would not classify myself exactly as a deist for a number of reasons, two of which I will comment on.

First, some deists hold the power of reason in highest regard. But reason itself ultimately concedes that love is the highest power, admitting itself to be a lesser authority. Second, most deist philosophers claim there is but one God. However, reason overrules this too, for ultimately we are all gods. This is because love is the highest authority and it can never be fully contained in any individual entity. Love is the absolute zenith in any realm of life. In other words, even one's creators are subject to the authority of love when directing us, or they would lose the right to lead us.

For these and many other reasons, I subscribe to no religion at all, simply being my own honest individual. Indeed, each of us is a religion unto ourselves. Reason itself ultimately concludes this too, showing us that love is the only universal denominator between us all.

That having been said, I would like to share with you some thoughts from a book titled The Age of Reason, by Thomas Paine, who called himself a Deist. I have also included an abridged and edited letter he wrote to a friend at the end of these excerpts.

Paine's thinking has shed a lot of light in dim places, especially regarding government as a younger man, then on religion in his twilight years. His first books literally helped lay the foundations of nations, but The Age of Reason, his last major work, will ultimately help lay the foundation of our world – a world which is coming to reject all religious fanaticism because of the pain and suffering it always causes, sooner or later.

The Age of Reason should be required reading for anyone who would dare proselytize his beliefs on another. I believe it is, in many ways, a more important book than the Bible – for anyone to whom the Bible is important. The same goes for the Koran, the Torah and Talmud, or any other man-made device which dares tell another person "what God says," or dictates to another person how to interact with their own god.

Paine's landmark work was written in two major sections, approximately two years apart, and more than two hundred years ago. His words herein are very abridged, and in many places I rearrange or paraphrase. I was exceedingly cautious to never change what he meant, even in the few places where I disagree in part.

Paine believed that all of us could communicate directly with our maker. His goal was to free his fellowman from the mental tyranny of organized religions. He said, "My own mind is my own church," and stressed that the true word of God was found in the creation itself, not in man made things like the scriptures.

The Age of Reason became famous throughout the United States and parts of Europe, and created a vicious backlash from organized religion which continued for years. Even today his work is reviled and suppressed by most clergy, for false workmen are humiliated by his logic. In fact, while the focus of Paine's book is on Christianity, using nothing more than common sense reasoning, he stunningly destroys the authority of any religion's scriptures as the "word of God," and leaves no doubt that the only true religion is between each of us and our god.

When Christian leaders verbally burned him at the stake for his honesty, Paine picked up his pen again, writing The Age of Reason – Part II. This time he challenged the authority of the Christian scriptures as the "word of God" by using the scriptures themselves! Again, he succeeded brilliantly, pointing out dozens of the multitude of inconsistencies and outright lies in these writings. And again, organized religions savagely railed against him in their shameful embarrassment.

Unable to win anything but the most trivial arguments with Paine, religious leaders fueled a vicious smear campaign that succeeded in having him shunned by most of society in the years that followed the two publications. Demonizing him with an endless stream of lies and slander, they continued their rabid tirades against his work for decades, long after his death. But his legacy lives on in the many truths he helped illuminate, while his detractors are long since forgotten.

Please note that my overview of Paine's book does not include quotes from the portions of Part II where he used just the scriptures to argue his points. Condensing these analyses to fit the limited space I have available might make them appear incomplete. You can find and read a complete version of his book on the Internet, freely available as part of the public domain. I hope you will take the time to do so.

This concludes my introduction to an unknown brother's work. Here then is my often paraphrased, very abridged and edited The Age of Reason, by Thomas Paine:

I believe in one God, and no more; and I hope for happiness beyond this life.

I believe in the equality of man, and that religious duties consist in doing justice, loving mercy, and endeavoring to make our fellow-creatures happy.

I do not believe in the creed professed by the Jewish church, by the Roman church, by the Greek church, by the Islamic church, by the Protestant church, nor by any church that I know of. My own mind is my own church.

All national institutions of churches appear to me as human inventions set up to terrify and enslave mankind, to monopolize power and profit.

I do not condemn those who believe otherwise; they have the same right to their belief as I have to mine. But it is necessary to the happiness of man that he be mentally faithful to himself. Infidelity does not consist in believing or disbelieving; it consists in professing to believe what he does not.

Every national church or religion has established itself by pretending some special mission from God, communicated to certain individuals. The Jews have their Moses; the Christians their Jesus Christ, their apostles and saints; and the Muslims their Mohammed; as if the way to God was not open to every man alike.

Each of those churches shows certain books, which they call revelation, or the Word of God. The Jews say that their Word of God was given by God to Moses face to face; the Christians say that their Word of God came by divine inspiration; and the Muslims say that their Word of God was brought by an angel from heaven. Each of those churches accuses the others of unbelief.

As for myself, I disbelieve them all.

* * *

The word revelation, when applied to religion, means something communicated immediately from God to man. No one will deny or dispute the power of the Almighty to make such a communication if he pleases. But admitting, for the sake of discussion, that something has been revealed to a certain person, it is revelation to that person only. When he tells it to a second person, a second to a third, and so on, it ceases to be a revelation to all those persons. It is revelation to the first person only, and hearsay to every other, and consequently, they are not obligated to believe it.

When Moses told the children of Israel that he received commandments from the hand of God, they were not obligated to believe him, because they had no authority but his telling them so; and I have no other authority for it than some historian telling me.

When I am told that the Koran was written in Heaven, and brought to Mohammed by an angel, the account is the same kind of hearsay evidence and secondhand authority as the former. I did not see the angel myself, and therefore have a right to reject it.

When I am told that a woman, called Virgin Mary, said she was pregnant without intercourse, and that her betrothed, Joseph, said an angel told him, I have a right to believe it or not. Such a circumstance requires a much stronger evidence than their word

116

for it, but we do not even have this, for it is only reported by others that they said so. It is hearsay upon hearsay, and I do not choose to rest my belief upon such evidence.

* * *

The Christian mythology presents Satan as making an insurrection and a battle in heaven, then being put into a pit, let out again, and then given a triumph over all creation when mankind was damned by eating an apple.

Putting aside laughter by its absurdity or detestation by its profaneness, it is impossible to conceive a story more derogatory to the Almighty.

In order to make a foundation for it to rise upon, the inventors gave Satan a power like the Almighty; for not only was Satan liberated from the pit, but afterwards his power increased to infinity. Before his fall he is an angel of limited existence, but afterwards he becomes omnipresent, meaning he exists everywhere, and at the same time.

Not content with this deification of Satan, they represent the Almighty as compelled to surrender the whole of creation to the sovereignty of this Satan, or come to earth and die.

That many good men have believed this strange fable, and lived very good lives, is without question. In the first place, they were educated to believe it, and they would have believed anything else if so indoctrinated. Also, many have been so enthralled by what they conceive to be the infinite love of God for man, in making a sacrifice of himself, that the vehemence of the idea has deterred them from truly examining the profaneness of the story.

Has the pride of man become so great that nothing can flatter it except the suicide of his Creator?

I know that this bold investigation will alarm many, but it will be a consolation to those under the burden of what to believe to see the subject freely investigated.

* * *

117

The books called the Bible, we are told, beginning with Genesis and ending with Revelations, are the words of God. It is therefore proper for us to ask who said so, that we may know better whether to credit such things. But the answer is, nobody knows.

The case, historically, is as follows: When the church mythologists established their system, they collected writings and managed them as they pleased. Whether the writings as now appear as the Old and the New Testament are in the same state in which those collectors say they found them, or whether they added, altered, abridged, or dressed them up is unknown.

Be this as it may, they decided by voting which books of the collection they had made should be the word of God, and which should not. They rejected several, voted some doubtful, such as the books called the Apocrypha, and those books which had a majority of votes are presented to us as God's official word.

*　*　*

It is not difficult to understand that credit was given to the story of Jesus Christ being the Son of God. He was born when the heathen mythology still had some fashion and repute in the world, and that mythology had prepared the people for the belief of such a story. However, the Jews, who had kept strictly to the belief of one God, always rejected the heathen mythology, and never credited the story.

It is interesting how doctrines of Christianity sprang out of the tail of the heathen mythology. A direct incorporation took place in the first instance, by making the reputed founder to be celestially begotten. The trinity of gods that then followed was no other than a reduction of the former plurality. The statue of Mary succeeded the statue of Diana of Ephesus. The deification of heroes changed into the canonization of saints. The Mythologists had gods for everything while the Christians had saints for everything. The church became as crowded with the one as the pantheon had been with the other, and Rome was the place of both. The Christian theory is little else than the idolatry of the ancient mythologists, accommodated to the purposes of power and revenue. Yet it remains to reason and philosophy to abolish the amphibious fraud.

Nothing that is said here applies, even with the most distant disrespect, to the real character of Jesus Christ. He was a virtuous and amiable man. The morality that he preached and practiced was of the most benevolent kind. Though similar systems of morality have been preached by many good men in all ages, it has never been exceeded by anyone.

But the stories of Jesus, relating to the supernatural parts, have every mark of fraud and imposition stamped upon them.

* * *

The parts of the Bible generally known by the name of the Prophets are the works of poets and itinerant preachers, who mixed poetry, anecdote, and devotion together.

There is not, in the whole Bible, any word that describes what we call a poet or poetry. The case is that the word prophet, to which later times have affixed a new meaning, was the Bible word for poet, and the word "prophesying" meant the art of making poetry or playing poetry to a tune upon a musical instrument.

The Bible speaks of prophesying with pipes and horns, of prophesying with harps and cymbals. If we now spoke of prophesying with a horn the expression would have no meaning, or appear ridiculous.

We are told of Saul being among the prophets, and also that he prophesied; but we are not told what was prophesied. The case is, there was nothing to tell, for this was a company of musicians and poets, and Saul joined in the concert, and this was called prophesying. But it appears that Saul prophesied badly, that is, he performed his part badly, for they say an "evil spirit from God came upon Saul, and he prophesied." (An evil spirit from God?!)

Now, were there no other passage in the book called the Bible, than this, to demonstrate we lost the original meaning of the word prophesy, and substituted another in its place, this alone would be sufficient; for it is impossible to apply the word prophesy in the place it is here used in the sense which later times have affixed to it.

The manner in which it is used here strips it of all religious meaning, and shows any man might be a prophet, or prophesy, as he may now be a poet or a musician, without any regard to his character.

Deborah and Barak are called prophets, not because they predicted anything, but because they composed the poem or song that bears their name. David is ranked among the prophets, for he was a musician, but Abraham, Isaac, and Jacob are not called prophets; and it does not appear from any accounts that they could sing, play music, or make poetry.

We are told of the greater and the lesser prophets. They might as well tell us of the greater and the lesser God, for there cannot be degrees in prophesying consistent with its modern sense. But there are degrees in poetry, and therefore the phrase is reconcilable to the case, when we understand it by the greater and the lesser poets.

* * *

If we permit ourselves to conceive right ideas of things, we must necessarily conclude the impossibility of change taking place in the Word of God; and therefore the Word of God cannot exist in any human speech or writing.

The continual change to which the meaning of words is subject, the lack of a universal language, which makes translations necessary, the errors to which such translations are subject, the mistakes of copyists and printers, together with the possibility of willful alterations, are of themselves evidence that human language, whether in speech or in print, cannot be the vehicle of the Word of God. The word of God exists in something else. It exists in the creation itself.

* * *

The Christian church has set up a system of religion very contradictory to the character of the person whose name it bears.

It has set up a religion of pomp and revenue in pretended imitation of a person whose life was humility and poverty.

The invention of a purgatory, the releasing of souls supposedly imprisoned there, by prayers, bought from the church with money, the selling of pardons, dispensations, and indulgences are all inventions by the church to collect money.

If I owe someone money and cannot pay him, another person can take the debt and pay it for me. But if I have committed a crime, every circumstance of the case is changed. Moral justice cannot take the innocent for the guilty even if the innocent would offer itself. To suppose justice to do this is to destroy the principle itself. This single reflection shows that the doctrine of redemption is yet another revenue collection idea, corresponding to debt which another person might pay.

I think man stands the same with his Maker as he ever did.

* * *

Some might say: Are we to have no word of God, no revelation? I answer: Yes! There is a Word of God; there is a revelation. The word of God is the creation we behold, and this is the word that no human invention can counterfeit or alter.

The Creation speaks a universal language, independent of human tongues, as various as they are. It is an ever existing original, which every man can read. It cannot be forged; it cannot be counterfeited; it cannot be lost; it cannot be altered; it cannot be suppressed. It does not depend upon the will of man whether it shall be published or not; it publishes itself from one end of the earth to the other.

* * *

Man understands in the meaning of God "first cause," that is, the cause of all things.

Incomprehensibly difficult as it is for a man to conceive what a first cause is, he believes it from the greater difficulty of disbelieving. It is indescribable to think that space can go on forever, but it is more difficult to conceive it ending. It is beyond the power of man to conceive eternity; but even harder to understand no time.

In like manner of reasoning, everything we behold carries in itself the internal evidence that it did not make itself. Every man is evidence to himself that he did not create himself; neither could his father make himself, nor his grandfather, nor any of his race; neither could any tree, plant, or animal make itself; and it is the conviction arising from this evidence that carries us by necessity to the belief of a first cause eternally existing.

This is a nature totally different to any material existence we know of, and by this power all things exist; and man calls this "God."

What more does man need to see to know that the power that made all these things is divine, is omnipotent? Believe this, and with a force impossible to deny a moral life will follow.

* * *

The Christian system of faith appears to me as a sort of denial of God. It is made up chiefly of man-ism, with little deism, and results in being as close to atheism as twilight is to darkness.

It introduces between man and his Maker an opaque body, which it calls a redeemer, just as the moon places itself between the earth and the sun; and it produces by this means an irreligious eclipse of light, which has put the whole orbit of reason into its shade.

Natural philosophy, embracing the whole circle of science, is the true study of the works of God, and is the true theology.

As to the theology that is now studied in its place, it is only the study of human opinions and fancies concerning God.

* * *

It is a fraud for the Christian system to call the sciences "human inventions." It is only the application of them that is human.

Man cannot make principles, he can only discover them. Every science has principles as fixed as those by which the universe is governed.

Man can make or draw a triangle, therefore it may be said that a triangle is a human invention. But the triangle, when drawn, is just the image of the principle. The triangle does not make the principle, any more than a candle taken into a dark room made the chairs that before were invisible. All the properties of a triangle exist independently of the figure, and existed before any triangle was thought of by man. Man had no more to do in the formation of those properties than he had to do in making the laws by which the heavens move, and so one must have the same divine origin as the other.

The Almighty lecturer, by displaying the principles of science in the structure of the universe, has invited man to study and imitate.

The advocates of the Christian system foresaw the knowledge that man would gain, with the aid of science, of the power and wisdom of God that is manifested in the structure and works of the creation, and that it would call into question the truth of their system of faith. Therefore it became necessary to their purpose to reject the study of science. They even persecuted it, and the age of scientific ignorance commenced with Christianity. It is almost impossible to believe that any religion would call it wickedness to seek to discover the structure of the universe that God had made, but the fact is too well established to be denied.

If we survey our world, we find every part of it filled and crowded with life, from the largest animals to the smallest insects the naked eye can see, and from there to others still smaller, totally invisible without a microscope. Every tree and plant, every leaf, serves not only as habitation, but as a world to some numerous life form.

Since no part of our earth is left unoccupied, why suppose that the immensity of space is a naked void, lying in eternal waste?

There is room for millions of worlds as large, or larger than ours, each of them millions of miles apart from each other.

In the midst of those reflections, what are we to think of the Christian system of faith?

I believe there have been men who persuaded themselves that a pious fraud, under some circumstances, might be productive of good. But the fraud once established could not afterwards be explained, begetting the calamitous necessity of going on. The people who first preached the Christian system of faith, combining it in some measure with the morality preached by Jesus, persuaded themselves it was better than the heathen mythology that then prevailed. But from the first preachers the fraud went on to the second, and to the third, until the idea of its being a pious fraud became lost in the belief of its being true; and that belief was further encouraged by the interest of those who made a livelihood preaching it.

But though such belief, by such means, might become common among the laity, it is next to impossible to explain the continual persecution carried on by the church against the sciences and its professors; except the church knows it cannot hold its power without such oppression, since the true word of God is self-evident when one contemplates the Creation itself.

* * *

I well remember, when about seven or eight years of age, hearing a sermon upon the subject of what is called Redemption by the death of the Son of God. After the sermon ended, I went into the garden, and as I was going down the garden steps (I perfectly remember the spot), I revolted at the recollection of what I had heard, and thought to myself that it was making God Almighty act like an emotional man, that he would kill his son when he could not avenge himself any other way.

This was not one of those kinds of thoughts that had any childish levity. It was to me a serious reflection, arising from the idea that God was too good to do such a thing, and too almighty to be under any necessity of doing so.

124

There are three principal means that religions employ to control mankind: Mystery, Miracle, and Prophecy.

With respect to Mystery, everything we behold is, in one sense, a mystery. Our own existence is a mystery, as is the whole vegetable world. We cannot account how an acorn, when put into the ground, is made to develop into an oak. But that it happens, we know for a fact, so it is not a mystery in this regard, even if the cause is unknown.

In the same sense, the word mystery cannot be applied to moral truth. Where it came from we do not know, but we know innately the correctness of moral truth, for a fact.

The very nature of religion proves it must be free from everything mysterious, for it must be to the comprehension of all. True religion is not learned like the secrets and mysteries of a trade, but rather by reflection. It arises out of the action of one's own mind upon the things which one sees, or upon what you may happen to hear or read, and the practice joins itself together.

But when men set up systems of religion incompatible with the word of God in the creation, they needed to invent a way to prevent questions, inquiries and speculations. The word mystery answers this purpose, and thus it has happened that religion, which is in itself without mystery, has been corrupted into a fog.

In the same sense that everything is a mystery, everything is a miracle, and no one miracle is greater than another. The elephant is not a greater miracle than a mite, nor is a mountain more miraculous than an atom. To an almighty power it is no more difficult to make one or the other, and no more difficult to make millions of worlds than one. Therefore, everything is a miracle in one sense, while in another, there is no such thing because it is only a miracle compared to our power and comprehension, but not a miracle to the power that performs it.

Mankind has observed certain laws by which nature is supposed to act, and calls it a miracle when something contrary takes place. But unless we know the whole extent of those laws and powers, we are not able to judge whether that which appears miraculous is within, or beyond, nature's natural ability to act.

Since appearances are so capable of deceiving, and things not real have a strong resemblance to things that are, it is inconsistent to suppose the Almighty would use miracles. It also implies what is preached could not stand on its own, degrading the Almighty into a showman.

Moreover, it is the most equivocal sort of evidence, for the credibility of any miracle rests solely on the reporter, and therefore it has the same chance of being believed whether true or false. Suppose I were to say, that when I sat down to write this book, a hand presented itself in the air, picked up the pen, and wrote every word; would anybody believe me? Would they believe me a whit more if it was a fact? Since a real miracle is subject to the same credibility doubts as a falsehood, the inconsistency becomes even greater to suppose the Almighty would use them, for it is more difficult to believe a miracle than obvious moral principle. Moral principle is self-evident and speaks universally as a word of God, all by itself.

As Mystery and Miracle took charge of the past and the present, Prophecy took charge of the future, and rounded the tenses of faith. It was not sufficient to know what had been done, but what would be done. The supposed prophet was the historian of times to come; and if he happened, in shooting with a long bow of a thousand years, to strike within a thousand miles of a mark, the ingenuity of posterity could make it a bulls-eye. And if he happened to be directly wrong, God had changed his mind.

It was shown earlier that the original meaning of prophet and prophesying has changed, and that a prophet, in the sense of the word now used, is a creature of modern invention. It is owing to this change in the meaning of the words, that the flights and metaphors of the Jewish poets, whose phrases and expressions have their original meanings obscured by the distance of time and culture, have been erected into prophecies, bent into explanations at the will and whimsical conceits of sectaries, expounders, and commentators. Everything unintelligible became prophetical, and even a blunder would serve for a prophecy, as anything unclear could be shaped into fact.

If by prophet, we mean one to whom the Almighty communicated some event that would take place in the future, either there were such people, or there were not. If there were, future events would be told in terms that could be understood, and not related in such an equivocal manner as to fit so many circumstances that might happen afterwards. It is conceiving very irreverently of the Almighty to suppose he would deal in this jesting manner with mankind.

But it is with Prophecy as with Miracle. It cannot answer the purpose even if it were real. Those to whom a prophecy was told could not tell whether the reporter was lying or not; and if the thing prophesied should happen, or something like it, among the multitude of things that are happening daily, nobody could know whether it was foreknown, or guessed, or whether it was accidental. A prophet is therefore useless and unnecessary.

On the whole, Mystery, Miracle, and Prophecy belong to the fictitious and not to true religion, and are tools by which religion has been made into a trade. The success of one impostor gave encouragement to another, and the quieting salvo of doing some good by keeping up a pious fraud protected them from remorse.

* * *

If I have already died in this body, and am raised again in the same body, it is presumptive evidence that I shall die again. This kind of resurrection is a gloomy doctrine.

As a matter of choice, as well as hope, I would rather have a more convenient form than the present. Every animal in the creation exceeds our abilities at something. Winged creatures pass over more space with greater ease than man. The smallest fish swims better than us beyond comparison and even the sluggish snail can ascend from the bottom of a pit.

The resurrection of the same body is far too little for all the powers and possibilities God has shown us.

Thought is of a different nature from everything else we know, and is essentially distinct from matter. A specific thought is eternally and identically the same. Every time that specific thought takes place, in whomever, or whatever, that thought has the capacity of existing unaffected by whatever combination of matter it resides in.

A thought therefore has in itself a capacity of being immortal, living wherever it is given a home, and living in as many homes as it is given.

It stands to reason then, that a producer of thoughts can also be immortal. Therefore, our own self-consciousness of existence, which produces its own thoughts, can be immortal and exist independent from matter we formerly occupied.

* * *

Man innately realizes the existence of an Almighty power. We know this for a fact though we cannot fully grasp the nature and manner of it. We also cannot conceive how we came here ourselves, yet we know for a fact that we are here. We must also know then, that the power that called us into being can call us to account for the manner in which we have lived here.

Were a man as fully and strongly impressed as he ought to be with the belief in God, he would stand in awe of God and his moral life would be regulated by the force of knowing that wrong behavior can never be concealed. To give this belief the full opportunity of growth, it is necessary that it act alone. This is deism.

If there ever was such a man as Adam, he was certainly a Deist. The only religion that has not been invented is pure and simple deism. But deism does not answer the purpose of despotic governments. They cannot lay hold of religion as an engine of power unless they mix it with human inventions and make their own authority a part. Neither does Deism answer the avarice of priests, who incorporate themselves and their functions with a religion and become, like the government, a party in the system.

Deism teaches us all which is necessary to be known, without the possibility of being deceived by others. The creation is the Bible of the deist. He reads there, in the hand-writing of his Creator, the immutability of God's power, the certainty of his own existence, and understands all man-made Bibles and Testaments are forgeries.

* * *

In summary, the idea or belief of a word of God existing in speech or writing is inconsistent, in itself. The reasons, among many others, are the lack of a universal language; the mutability of language; the errors to which translations are subject, the possibility of suppressing such a word; the probability of altering it, or of fabricating the whole and imposing it upon the world.

The Creation we behold is the real and ever existing word of God, in which we cannot be deceived. It proclaims his power, it demonstrates his wisdom, and it manifests his goodness and beneficence. The moral duty of man consists in imitating this.

I am not worried about my future existence. I am content with believing, even certain, that the power that gave me existence is able to continue it, in any form and manner he pleases, either with or without this body; and it appears to me more probable that I shall continue to exist hereafter than that I was brought into existence in the first place.

It is certain that, in one point, all nations of the earth and all religions agree – all believe in a God. The things in which they disagree are the man-made additions annexed to that belief; and therefore, if ever a universal religion should prevail, it will not be by believing anything that is not already known to us all.

All my detractors resort, more or less, to what they call Scripture Evidence and Bible authority, to help them out. They are so little masters of the subject that they confuse a dispute about authenticity as a dispute about doctrines. Anything may be claimed to be proved from the Bible, but before the Bible can be admitted as proof, the Bible itself must be proved, for if the Bible is not true, it ceases to have authority and proves nothing.

It has been the practice of all Christian commentators, priests, and preachers, to impose the Bible on the world as a mass of truth, the word of God. They have disputed and wrangled, and anathematized each other about the supposed meaning of parts and passages therein. One has insisted that such a passage meant one thing, another that it meant directly the contrary, and a third that it meant something different from both; and this they call understanding the Bible. The answers I have seen in reply to me have been written by these pious men, and like their predecessors, they contend and wrangle, and in understanding the Bible; each understands it differently, but each understands it best; and they agree on nothing but in telling their readers that Thomas Paine understands it not.

Now instead of wasting their time in fractious disputes about doctrinal points drawn from the Bible, these men ought to know, and if they do not it is polite to inform them, that the first thing to be understood is, whether there is sufficient authority for believing the Bible to be the word of God, or whether there is not? Plainly there is not.

There are matters in that book, said to be done by the express command of God, that are as shocking to humanity as any wickedness ever done by man. When we read in the books ascribed to Moses, Joshua, etc., that the Israelites came upon whole nations who they put to the sword, not sparing the elderly, not even the infants, that they left not a soul alive, are we really to believe that it was God who commanded these things!

* * *

Paine's Letter to a Friend

In your letter you cite quotations from the Bible, which you call the "word of God," to show my opinions on religion are wrong. However, I could give you as many, from the same book, to show yours are wrong, so consequently, the Bible decides nothing as it decides any way we choose. But by what authority do you call the Bible the "word of God?" This is the first point to be settled.

130

It is not your calling it so that makes it true, any more than the Muslims calling the Koran the "word of God" makes that true. Popish councils voted the books that now comprise the New Testament to be the "word of God." This was done by yeas and nays, as we vote a law. The Pharisees of the second Temple did the same with the books that comprise the Old Testament. And this is all the authority there is, which is no authority at all. I am as capable of judging for myself as they were, and I think more so, because they made a living by their religion, so they had an interest in the vote they made.

You may think a man is inspired, but you cannot prove it. The same is the case with the word "revelation." There can be no evidence of such a thing, so you can no more prove revelation than you can prove what someone dreams.

It is said in the Bible that God spoke to Moses, but how do you know? Because, you say, the Bible says so. The Koran says that God spoke to Mohammed, do you believe that too? No. Why not? Because, you will say, you do not believe it. And so, because you do, and because you do not, is all the reason you can give for believing or disbelieving, except that you will say that Mohammed was an impostor. And how do you know Moses was not an imposter? As for me, I believe all are impostors who pretend to hold verbal communication with the Deity.

The case is, you form your opinion of God from the account of him in the Bible; and I form my opinion of God from the wisdom and goodness manifested in the structure and the works of the Creation.

The result is, by taking the Bible for your standard, you arrive at a bad opinion of God; but by taking God as manifested in the Creation for my standard, I form a bad opinion of the Bible.

The Bible represents God to be a changeable, emotional, vindictive Being; making a world, then drowning it, afterwards repenting, and promising not to do so again. He sets one nation to cut the throats of another, then stops the sun till the butchery is done. But the works of God in the Creation preach a different doctrine. In that vast volume, we see nothing to give us the idea of a changeable, emotional, vindictive God. Everything we see there impresses us with a contrary idea – that of eternal order, harmony, and goodness. The sun and the seasons return at their appointed times, and everything in the Creation proclaims that God is unchangeable.

Now, which "word of God" should I believe? One is a book that any impostor might make, but the other is the Creation itself, which none but an Almighty Power could make. The Bible says one thing and the Creation says another. The Bible represents God like a mortal, but the Creation proclaims him with all the attributes of a God.

That bloodthirsty man, called the prophet Samuel, makes God to say, (i Sam. xv. 3), "Now go and smite Amalek, and utterly destroy all that they have, and spare them not, but slay both man and woman, infant and suckling, ox and sheep, camel and ass." That Samuel or another impostor might say this, is what, at this distance of time, cannot be proved or disproved, but in my opinion, it is blasphemy to say, or to believe, that God decreed it. All our ideas of the justice and goodness of God revolt at such impious cruelty. It is not a God, just and good, but a devil, under the name of God, that the Bible describes!

What makes this pretended order to destroy the Amalekites appear even worse, is the reason given for it. The Amalekites, 400 years before, according to the account in Exodus XVII (but which appears to be a fable from the magical account of Moses holding up his hands), had opposed the Israelites coming into their country. This the Amalekites had a right to do, because the Israelites were invaders. And this opposition by the Amalekites, at that time, is given as a reason, that everyone, born four hundred years afterwards, should be put to death. And to complete the horror, Samuel chopped the leader of the Amalekites in to pieces.

This slaughter was done by the express command of God? I will never believe any book that ascribes cruelty and injustice to God, and reject the Bible as unworthy of credit.

As I have now given some of my reasons for believing the Bible is not the word of God, I ask your reasons for believing the contrary. But I know you can give none, except you were educated to believe the Bible; and as the Muslims have the same reason for believing the Koran, it is evident that education makes all the difference, and that reason and truth have nothing to do with it. You believe the Bible from the accident of birth, and the Muslims believe the Koran from the same accident, and each calls the other "infidel." But leaving the prejudice of education aside, all are infidels who believe falsely of God.

When you have examined the Bible honestly, for I do not think you have, and permit yourself to really think about "God," then you will probably believe as I do. But this letter is not written to change your opinion, but rather to satisfy you, and some other friends whom I esteem, that my disbelief of the Bible is because of my genuine belief in God.

*   *   *

This concludes the excerpts from The Age of Reason.

Personal

Creation

In the beginning, it was nothing, it felt nothing, except that it was somehow conscious of being nothing, though it did remember excruciating pain that had slowly faded away into the nothing that it had become. With exceedingly great sorrow, the last thought it had was "I am nothing."

Then, suddenly, "I am," he thought to himself. He looked at himself and rejoiced; "I am, I am like a god," he said. "I am like a god, I am like a great god," he shouted.

There was another Presence with him, but he could not comprehend it, for he was thinking how glorious he was. The spirit tried to speak to him, but he was too busy beholding the glory in himself to listen, "I am like a great god, I will be like the greatest god," he boasted!

Every member of the Eternal was trying desperately to reach him now, in hope of somehow saving him, but he could not be stopped. Magnifying himself exceedingly, he proclaimed, "I will be like the greatest god; I will be even greater!" He was wondering if such a thing was possible as he vanished from their presence.

The next thing he knew he was ruling over a world with absolute authority. No creature was his equal, and he alone was great. But the joy he felt in this was brief and faded almost immediately, and was quickly replaced by profound loneliness that was utterly consuming him, and his unequaled greatness was no comfort at all. Finally, he could no longer bear it; his soul in utter anguish over his aloneness, he cried out, "O, God, I wish I had someone like me to be with."

Instantly, his God appeared to comfort his aching spirit, and he remembered that this lonely world had all been a lesson he had needed. Lovingly, his God asked, "How about we get you a companion?" "Yes," he answered happily.

He will recall later that one of his members hoped he could have this companion without allowing for equality, and then others among his members hoped this, too.

"All right, I need you to fall asleep," God said. This seemed strange to him because he perceived it to be a nonexistence, so he questioned it. In fact, it seemed so strange a request that he questioned going to sleep two more times. But each time he did, God assured him with a faith he knew he could trust, so he willed himself to sleep.

He will later remember a few unusual things that happened while he was sleeping though, and they were revelations to him when they were recollected. First, he worried that his companion might rule over him, but God reassured him immediately. But then he again hoped he might somehow have a companion and yet rule over this coming friend. After this happened, he asked his God, "Can I have two companions?" to which God replied, "No." Yet his desire for two companions was so strong that he asked God over and over again, certain that one would not be enough. Six times he asked and received "No" for an answer, but the seventh time he asked, God stopped and paused to think about something.

He also remembered that he was somehow now outside of himself and able to watch himself thinking. As he beheld the vast expanse of nothingness (except it had some luminescence to it) from which God was about to make his companion, he genuinely doubted such a thing was possible (understand, he was beholding himself). "How can something come from nothing?" he wondered. "My friend will never be able to be my equal?" he wondered to himself. (Later he realized he was wrong, for he was the same thing she was being made from.)

The next thing he knew he awoke, and what an awakening it was! Pure Joy! That is what happened next! He had someone just like himself to be with! They rejoiced exceedingly as they raced all around their world, discovering the treasures within it, and everything one of them found was immediately and completely shared with the other! What ecstatic delight! He never knew such incredible happiness was possible!

How long this joy lasted he did not know, only that it was perfect and complete without any exception. But he did recall, just before it ended, that his friend was thinking and acting in a way he had never seen. He wondered why that was and then his friend was standing before him holding that which was forbidden, and offering it to him. He accepted, knowing he should not, but he rationalized he could make the excuse that his friend offered it to him, though he knew it did not excuse him. The truth is that he was just curious, just like his friend had been.

The great joy they once held was gone immediately. Instead of sharing everything like they once did, now they were deciding which of them should possess what, though nothing was very interesting any more. Back and forth they went, calmly deciding who should claim each particular thing as their own, when suddenly, "It's mine!" his friend shouted, latching hold of something. "What is it?" he exclaimed, as he too grabbed hold of it. "It's mine!" his friend shrieked. "No, I want it!" he screamed. "What is it?" he demanded angrily. They wrestled furiously for possession of it, neither of them relenting. "It's mine!" his friend screamed at him. "What is it?" he demanded with incredible fury, lamenting from his heart that God should make his companion stop refusing to answer his question. "It's the ability to reproduce ourselves," his friend immediately answered him.

"I want it!" he yelled. "No!" the answer shot back, as the frenzied battle raged on, both of them fighting with all of their might. But he could not prevail; his friend broke away with possession of it, and he wailed in bitter grief.

He stopped crying when their God appeared to find out what was wrong. Soon, he and his friend were shouting blame at one another. She tried to crush his spirit by saying that since she won the fight for possession of it, she was therefore stronger and better than him. Her words cut bitterly into his soul and he was utterly heartbroken. But God immediately comforted him, and rebuked her, asking, "Is it not better to give than to receive?" She was humbled by God's words and stopped her arrogance immediately, as she worried if her companion might be better than her. When he then realized that he possessed the "give" of having children, while she possessed the "receive," he tried to crush her spirit by saying that he was stronger and better than her because of it. His words cut bitterly into her soul, and when he saw that she was utterly heartbroken, he told her that his sin was her fault, to which she despaired of living any more. God now turned to comfort her.

God then left them so they would be alone together, in hopes that they would choose to forgive each other, first trying hard to convey to them that they were still equals and should love each other.

139

Still hurt and angry, at first they told each other more lies about what would come to pass for each other, their selfish wills pressing hard to hurt each other.

But they were unable to deny their truest feelings. Slowly the love they felt for each other began to reappear, and when they finally repented of their selfishness they began moving towards each other, soon finding themselves racing towards their joyful reunion. The newest eternal member of the spirit of love was about to be born.

The 7th Day

Once upon an infinite number of times a beloved child was reflecting on what was happening as it was taking place and realized while playing with his and her toys that creating things with them was possible and so was like a god proclaiming I am to these things and having never been in control of anything before proclaimed authority not just over what they had created but over all creations ever which was soon discovered that while halfway a fact in their new world was but childishness even foolishness to everyone else but he and she insisted on dominion over all things and so they were set outside all alone for a moment so the child could see how it really looked for he and she were even claiming to have begot the very parents they originated from and so now all alone they asked themself who am I and beholding their answer in themself did not understand why they were only equals instead of over all as the future suggested it had a way to keep them above all else but he and she later repented of wanting such total dominion while nearly dying from shame as earlier gods remembered their own early days for though having forgotten now remembered the lessons they too had first learned bless this little child him and her and welcome home they said to their children as soon as you are able they spoke from their heart and thank you for reminding us these other members of the spirit spoke from their hearts as they picked up the boy and girl who had died and broken in two in seeking to be above all and encouraged them to stop hurting each other and reunite and though the boy and girl were fearful they would be hurt again and still wanted to be above each other in their selfishness they decided to move towards equality even trying to share each other's temples as a gesture of love but just as physical babies fall before walking so it is with spiritual babies but they were not ashamed but instead happy at the small gain and so they had truly begun trying to accept equality to each other and this time they were able to stand and though still apart struggling to accept their obvious equality they had moved closer and though not walking in agreement yet were encouraged by the gain so took another step towards each other and the pain of having fallen was swallowed in the joy of having moved towards each other in true friendship as walking turned into running towards their reunion of flight...

141

A Common Problem

About everyone I knew, and everyone I met, I said in my heart, "I am better than you." Even worse, I was sure of it most of the time, and on the rare occasions when I was not, I would seethe with jealously and immediately look for a way to believe I was better. It was not enough for me to be an equal – I wanted to be above you.

Sadly, I confess that this is no story I am telling here, but rather my true confession.

Two plus eight equals ten, three plus seven equals ten, four plus six equals ten. A child could see that different components can equal the same total. But I wanted anyone different to be inferior, and so I tried, wallowing in the quagmire of spiritual fractions until I arrived at zero, for myself.

I could hang my head in shame, but I am not alone, because it is, or was, everybody's biggest problem, everybody's strongest demon. We call it pride, and what a giant-size demon it is, the king of them all, for though Satan lived in heaven, he was nevertheless cast out for his sin. And what was that sin? He was exceedingly proud of himself, to the point that he magnified himself above all others, even above the collective one God. In other words, he said he was greater than all the other infinite number of Gods combined – the very spirit itself.

In view of this, it is easy to understand the tremendous size of our own human pride, in our spiritual youth, which always says in its heart, "I am better than you."

No wonder the old law said, "All who see God's face must die."* For what does God's face look like? Your very own reflection in a mirror! Such is the incomprehensible love felt for us by the spirit that we should have equality with the almighty available to us at all times. But babies, self-centered, and self-righteous, cannot bear to share anything, not even that which they were given.

The fact remains, however, that there is simply no fitting place for arrogance – not in this current age, and most certainly not in the next age. So we should always keep an eye on cultivating the good fruits of the spirit in ourselves. But until that new age comes for us, we need to be working day to day in this temporary illusion we call "time," learning to love one another, and trying to rid ourselves of pride and all the other foolish and evil thoughts with which our hearts and minds seem to be continually occupied.

We know that the spirit can appear in any form. Knowing that nothing is hidden from them, and that our very thoughts, if from the heart, can actually be heard by them, what kind of impression do you think we usually make?

*Note: Our spiritual growth at the time this old law was given ("All who see God's face must die.") shows us how spiritually childish the people (represented by Moses) and the spirit of Jesus were back then. They were so jealous to witness an indisputable equal (at the very least) that they would search for any flaw in order to justify killing this other being.

Two other examples of this kind of spiritual immaturity come to mind. One is shown in the interaction between Job and his lord in a situation of being "face to face" (in a sense), when all Job cared about was destroyed, except his wife. Another was when Jacob was spitefully crippled by the angel of his Lord after Jacob wrestled with him and neither could prevail.

Voices

On two different occasions, both many years ago when I was a young man, I heard a voice speak directly to me from thin air. The spirit leads me not to retell the exact words I heard (it would be irrelevant, for they were parables intended privately for me), but the essence of the words on the first of these occasions was to tell me that I was a better person than most other people.

What arrogance I possessed, to hear the long-standing desire of my innermost heart spoken aloud. This is now very embarrassing to me, for it plainly shows the profound conceit I once harbored, and a love for myself far above all others. It also indicates some mental illness, for want of a better term, though anyone who is not ruled by love is very sick indeed. Also, note that it does not indicate some illness because I heard the voice, but because I was more flattered than I was repulsed by the lie. However, as I see the potential to do some good with it, I am relating to you what is humiliating for me.

You see, the desire to be above my fellow man had been an overwhelming desire for me since early in my youth. But the arrogance, conceit, hatred and other useless fruit of worthless spirits was at long last weakening before the silent voice of the true spirit of life. "Time to give up this childishness; love is the answer" it always said. And this is why the voice came – a demon's desperation to hold on to me. In other words, the satan in me was losing its grip. I was finally conceding in my heart that my own puny wisdom was inferior to the infinitely greater wisdom of the everlasting spirit, and its eternal call to love each other.

The second instance was a disparaging comment regarding my wife's character, just after we were married. The details are not important, since the gist of it all is simply that the comment was true when viewed from one small perspective, but was actually an enormous lie. This I did not discover until years later, when I had grown wise enough to see a much bigger picture.

Bottom line: Never trust a spirit voice spoken out loud. Even if the words seem true, the intent surely has some evil in it, which time will reveal. The pure spirit speaks in silence. Its voice is clear and true, heard in the heart with never a need to ripple the air, for sinless spirit does not need the physical to be heard.

Many have gone astray having heard voices, even going so far as to commit murder. Truly this is a place where one's very light is darkness, so blind, so sick in the soul that they hope wicked deeds will somehow supply proof that God holds them superior to others.

Others get close to that sick. Abraham, the patriarch of the people responsible for three of the world's most historically violent religions, nearly ruined his own spiritual odyssey, considering whether or not to obey a demon's voice that told him to murder his son. A man who set out to do such a thing today would rightfully be removed from society. However, long ago, the practitioners of priestcraft reshaped the near folly as proof of Abraham's superiority.

Though Abraham was a man who cared deeply about spiritual things, and therein was his merit, a proper way to retell the story is that it proves his great immaturity at the time, for he considered the invisible voice from his and Sarah's egos might be more important than the child from their heart.

Then there's Moses, who was also a man with some merit, but sick in the soul, proved by his vicious over-punishment of a cruel man by murdering him.

Yet these are the kind of people from whom we are all descended, spiritually speaking. Who among us is not self-righteous at heart, sometimes cruel and unforgiving? But the spirit will lead us to love, if only we let it.

Thankfully, it is not just the presently lost that comprise the "to Everlasting" that we live among, for a multitude of the "from Everlasting" is here as well. We just have a harder time seeing them in our arrogance.

Removing a Speck

Jesus said, "First remove the log from your own eye, then you can see clearly how to remove the speck in your neighbor's eye."

After many years of behaving like a pharisee in such matters, I finally learned what Jesus meant. It means that we should try to remove the speck from our neighbor's eye so that what we have done was unnoticed by them.

This is very hard to do though, but not because of our neighbor. It is because of us; for while the spirit will often immediately provide us the directions for success, our own nature wants desperately to draw attention to the good work we were attempting, so as to be "above our fellow man." Notice I said "were" attempting, because if we draw attention to our help, then our work is immediately wounded, maybe even dead. People go deaf and blind to almost anything said or done with conceit.

What if there honestly seems to be no way to remove the speck unnoticed? Then perhaps question that person's behavior directly with gentle words, or a mere questioning look. But remember to do it with love and in humility. Harshness is seldom called for. This having been said, we usually need to double check ourselves first, to be sure doing anything at all is proper.

A common reason we are often unable to see a way to help, indeed exceedingly common, is because the spirit wants us to mind our own business. The timing or situation might be wrong to involve ourselves. Even more often, our perceptions of another person's errors are mistaken, our judgment having been clouded by our own inequities or incomplete understanding. In other words, in the vast majority of situations, people lack the ability to correctly judge the visible actions of someone else's heart and soul. We can barely manage our own affairs.

Lastly, oftentimes the best way to remove a speck is simply by setting a good example. People do notice how others behave and it does make an impact. Besides, just like us, the spirit is always working to help our neighbors grow.

But when we do try to help, we need to remember to be silent about the whole thing, or at least as gentle as possible. Sometimes it helps to talk about our own sins or mistakes so an existing or potential friend can listen without being on the defensive.

Above all, we do not want to behave like a pharisee, imagining and acting as though we are better. This always deafens another person's ability to hear a different perspective.

The truth is that we all take turns helping each other.

A Wise and Gentle Rebuke

One night as I lay sleeping, (I did not know I was sleeping at the time), I was in the vast expanse of the From Everlasting and able to communicate with all of the other members of the spirit who are ruled by the authority of love.

My nature being what it was, I wanted to gauge my depth of wisdom (spiritually speaking), compared to the other members of this great collective spirit. So I determined to survey them, asking a number of them if I held a higher level of understanding than they possessed. I soon realized my question did not make sense to anyone I asked. Indeed I was speaking total gibberish in their minds, so I resolved to find another way to get an answer.

What I came up with was quite clever, for I simply asked each entity a question, the essence of which was: "Were you here when I arrived?" To my chagrin, every member, one after another, answered, "Yes." And although I cannot explain how such a thing is possible, I polled every one of them.

This of course made me quite despondent, as I lamented to myself that spiritually speaking, "I am the youngest one here."

Almost immediately after taking that true conclusion to heart, another member of the spirit appeared next to me. He leaned over my shoulder and whispered into my ear with noticeable conceit, "That's right; you're the youngest one here."

I cheered up a bit, and was a little wiser.

Another Wise and Gentle Rebuke

Some streams of thoughts are good and others are evil, but most are a combination of both good and evil in varying proportions. It is the same way with dreams and visions, so it is important to examine the spirits here, too. And though dreams and visions will always be of a far lesser value than actual events, since they are destined to pass away as prophecy has, they nevertheless can be of occasional value.

The time it takes to understand the important meanings of a dream or vision, if there are any, (usually there is not), can range from immediately to many years. We can even feel sure we understand them only to discover we did not, since they are so often lies, or partly lies, or in the form of parables, which is how Jesus often spoke. On rare occasions though, the true meaning of a dream or vision, or at least a part of the meaning, is clear immediately. Here is one that happened to me:

One night as I was sleeping, I was preaching to a room full of people. (I did not know I was dreaming at the time.) In the course of my sermon, I mentioned that I did not eat very much meat since the practice seems rather violent to me, was not allowed until after sin, and will not exist in the world to come, a world where "nothing shall hurt or kill."

As I was speaking, the spirit was trying to get my attention to provide me a little help. This was not because I was not making any sense, but because what I was saying was being construed by the congregation as the lord having forbid such a thing. Furthermore, the topic is less important than so many other issues in this age.

But I would not heed the spirit's counsel. Being conceited about my position and understanding, I continued to talk on and on about this topic against my lord's wishes, instead of moving on to something of importance. I was just having so much fun confounding the congregation with my unanswerable arguments that I persisted. "After all," I continued my discourse, "Which is greater, the distance between man and the animals, or the distance between man and God?"

This final question was impossible for my congregation to answer, so they sat there confounded in silence. But to my shocking surprise, there rose up from thin air and appeared in the midst of them a messenger from

God, and he had an angry answer that left me speechless instead. The messenger said: "The greatest distance is man to man!"

It was such a memorable lesson, and in a dream no less. To this day I believe it only needs "man to man" replaced with "person to person" to make the wisdom in the messenger's words perfect.

You Reap What You Sow

After many years of denying the truth about my behavior, I was exhausted from the spiritual beating I had inflicted on myself. So I asked God to help and soon found myself blessed in a number of ways. Then disaster struck – my wife took ill and died. Afterwards, I was so devastated that I could barely get from one day to the next. This was truly the saddest time of my life.

I could end the story here and hope you would feel sorry for me, as if I suffered unjustly, or as if my road is harder to travel than yours is, or has been, or will be. However, this is not the case.

The truth is that the profound sorrow I have suffered by having my wife die was what I required, for my heart was setting on self. Because of this, and her similar behavior, our spiritual growth kept slowing, and this tragedy happened primarily as a last resort for us. Indeed, we wished such heartbreak on each other. Painfully small we were for each other, spiritually speaking.

Many people remind me of the way I once was. Dishonest with themselves, their conversations about their trials and tribulations are geared to solicit the listener's praise for their character. In self-righteous darkness they blindly refuse to accept they will never convince anyone of their imaginary superiority, least of all their beloved reflection. When it comes to problems or unhappiness that originated from a spiritual cause, many people insist they had little or nothing to do with it. But that is foolishness. If you have a problem or sorrow and the origin is spiritual, then you either share the blame, or are to blame.

Small Miracle

Years ago, before my wife and I married, we were intimate with each other, which resulted in her becoming pregnant. Even though I should have married her (because I knew she was the one for me, not because she was pregnant), I insisted she get an abortion. My reasoning was because she had secretly stopped using birth control and had intentionally gotten pregnant. I did not want us to marry under this pretense.

As it happens, during this time I was employed as a taxi driver. This particular occupation provided me with lots of time to do nothing but think, since whenever business was slow I just sat there reflecting on what a shambles I had made of my life. As you might guess, one of the things I had been spending time thinking about was the abortion. Even with my beloved's deception, the genuine love that already existed between us should have given me cause to forgive her and accept the child. Under these circumstances I should not have asked her to get an abortion. After all, and I admit this to my shame – I knew she was my soul mate. She deceived me, so I was not wrong, but a better course of action was there if I could have seen it. Sadly, my heart was too hard.

Now in the course of my employment one day, I was sent to pick up a fare at one of the local churches. I remember thinking that it was an odd place for a fare, and especially so, since it was not a day for services.

When I arrived at the church, no one was there and the doors were locked. Bewildered, I got back in the car and sat down behind the wheel when I heard something behind me. I turned around to see a boy getting into my car. Where he came from I do not know, since I was just looking in that direction, but I just shrugged it off and asked him where he wanted to go.

He looked cold and distant, unfriendly, and did not even look at me when I asked where he was going. I said "hi" to him but he still never looked at me and said not a word. It was as though he did not hear me. Then I noticed he was holding an envelope, which had an address written on the outside. I politely took it from him since he could not seem to hear me, read the address, and started to drive. I looked at him again, trying to make some kind of contact, but he continued to ignore me, or could not hear me, and just kept staring straight ahead out the window.

Silently we drove along. Yet again I thought to start a conversation, but he did not speak, and so I just kept quiet myself, unsure as to whether he was ignoring me or actually could not see or hear me.

As we drove along to his destination, I found my thoughts returning over and over again to the abortion. I could not help thinking about it, and somehow I knew that something strange and marvelous was happening at that very moment.

I was completely immersed in these thoughts as I turned the car into the driveway of the address on the envelope and parked. Shutting the meter off, I realized the fare was exactly the amount in the envelope, and would have been amazed by that except that I somehow expected it. As he got out of the car, I silently watched him as he walked up the driveway towards the house, overwhelmed by the knowledge that this was the child we had aborted, and I really longed to say something to him.

Immediately he stopped and turned around to look at me. For the first time our eyes met, and I no longer saw the anger or unfriendliness in his face, only detachment, like when two strangers look at one another. Then the most amazing thing happened – he spoke to me with his mind, for his mouth never moved and my ears never heard it, but I heard his voice inside my brain as clear as if a person standing next to me had spoken! I still remember the exact words he said to me: "You're forgiven, which is not to say you have approval."*

I was stunned! His words were ringing in my mind as he turned again and walked to the house, and I drove away lost in amazement.

But this is still not the end. Afterwards, reflecting and marveling over what I had witnessed, I decided to drive back to revisit the house. Not as if I did not believe what had happened, but to relive it, for I was lost in wonderment. I drove down the road and turned down the street where it happened, and there to my astonishment, the house was not there! To this very day I remember the address.

* The way the boy really felt was that he had not forgiven me, but conceded I was right. However, with the benefit of hindsight you see how I feel about it now.

Sunset

That a person would pray for death might seem impossible to some people, especially when young and healthy, but it was right for me at the time (many years ago). I saw it as a way to repair the damage I had caused and I had hopes of finding joy by it. After all, the caterpillar that crawls may someday come to fly, and so it is that the person who repents and accepts the authority of Love and Equality has much to look forward to.

But this courage to cross over while young and healthy was not the brave thing it might appear to be, for it only came from the shame and repentance I felt at having discovered how small a person I was. Would you believe that I quietly rejoiced to learn my wife was seriously ill? And until an hour before she died I did not truly care.

Fortunately, I came to my senses at the last moment and hoped she would not die. But, it was not enough to change the fact that I needed to learn a hard and painful lesson. And so a part of me died as I held her in my arms and helplessly watched her take her last breath. My heart was broken.

How did I get in such a position, why did I stop caring about her? The details are not important; every love affair has a story. Basically, it was just that she had wronged me many times. But what about my own behavior? What makes it even worse is that we were best friends.

Immediately after she died my course was clear – I would pursue our reunion. Jesus said that even if we were standing at the very altar itself, if we remembered our brother had some grievance against us then we must "go away; first be reconciled to your brother, then come back and offer your gift." This makes perfect sense to me.

Naturally, the satan in me relentlessly argues with my course of action, constantly reminding me of my wife's injuries to me – but this is the kind of thinking that tripped me up in the first place – for what about my own sins? What a fool, blindly concluding that my spiritual twin was somehow less than myself since her sins were different than mine.

Two and eight make ten. Three and seven make ten. A child could see that different components can equal the same total. But I would not listen. Since she is my spiritual twin, she only did what I would have if I had lived her life. What a hypocrite I was.

This was the rational that led me to pray for death, though I see now, years later with the benefit of hindsight, that I only needed to pray for reunion. The spirit will work out the best way to fix things.

About four years later I received what I believed was a clear answer that my prayers had been granted, so consequently I set about to put my affairs in order. The first of which was this book for our young son, that he might know us a little better, and to make mention of some things I knew he would understand in time. In the process, I found myself writing parts of it for my wife, as a means of reaching out to her, and soon found myself writing even more for anyone who cares to read it, hoping some might benefit from the experiences I share.

Then, having completed the book, I put it away safely and waited patiently, as the time for my passing was to be very soon. This essay and many others were added years later.

I do not fully understand, but apparently I was deceived, or something else happened, for the time came and went, but I remained. How could this have happened I wondered? I was thoroughly depressed and felt very much let down. Disappointed, I gave up my commitment to strive for immediate reunion with my wife and set about to return to a more regular life again.

But I still had hopes of reunion someday, so I prayed with all sincerity for a small favor – that God would let me know by way of a sign when I was about to die. Not just any sign, but a very specific request was what I asked for, so that when the day came that I saw it, I would recognize it without a doubt. And I promised that even if it was 40 years before he answered, that I would remember what I had this day asked for. Understand, I did not ask for a sign to believe, but only to keep from being cruelly fooled again, so my conscious is clear.

Here is an amazing thing: Not a single week went by, but miracle, I beheld my special and private sign. Not 40 years did I have to wait, but only 4 days. I was forgiven and was headed home for our reunion. I renewed my faith and waited patiently.

But it was not to be. My imminent death never happened. The days turned into weeks, then months, as I again waited in vain, experiencing the cruelest illusion of them all. I had asked in genuine faith and I swear on my very salvation that I beheld the sign.

What kind of test is this? That was the question as time went by and my disappointment turned to anger. But I had no answer.

Perhaps it was to see if I would do wrong if I believed God had wronged me? But I will not. I have learned my lesson about sin. Or perhaps I was allowed to sit in God's seat, so to speak, like Job was, and in so doing found these results. Whatever the causes, the main reason it appears that God failed me is because I am the only one that can accomplish the goal I have set. No one else may do it for me. My parents, their parents, indeed, all the members of the spirit "from everlasting" stand to the side ceaselessly encouraging me, but the work is mine alone to do. For my satan has argued that if I really believe, I will do it even if I have to do it alone. (And so it is he sets his own future by his judgments today, which are the kind of mistakes I know about).

But I take heart in knowing that at least darkness is past for me, and wherever I am in this age, (I do not know because it is not important), I do know that I will carry on.

And the answer for "what to do now" remains the same, regardless of the obstacles. I will seek our reunion, if only to apologize for my poor behavior towards a true friend. Not by doing nothing with my time but studying and reflecting, but by living my life one day at a time and learning more about love and equality, confident that in so doing my heart will make the necessary changes so my wife and I can be friends again.

I honestly believe that nothing is happier than genuine friendship.

Friends

With the exception of Christianity, I understood very little of any other religion. In my mind they did not make sense, for I was overwhelmed with amazement of Jesus. If Jesus does not fit the description of enlightened, who does? Has anyone ever spoken with such wisdom and understanding? These are the kinds of questions I put to my friends about Jesus because this is the way I felt about him. Now I know better, but I am still filled with admiration for him. And I will follow his final commandment forever.

I wondered how the Jews, Muslims, and others rejected Jesus' divinity, yet plainly acknowledge he existed, deeming him only a teacher or prophet. Many others credit Jesus with nothing at all, except that he was a person. These beliefs, and many others, go against traditional Christian dogma, but nevertheless they are absolutely correct, and beautifully so at that.

There are a number of ways by which their cases could be argued. But since true religion is ultimately completely personal, I will instead share a very personal experience, which for me goes right to the heart of the matter.

Many years ago, I tried to strike up a conversation with a man that I thought was a stranger, unaware that I was speaking to an angel. Early in the conversation I asked him his opinion of some particular scriptures, but with genuine friendship he immediately stopped me with this astounding rebuke. He simply stated, "I already have a wife." I will not digress with further commentary on the incident, except to note that my own wife was always seeing Christ in other people, so the correction was exceedingly clever.

But there is a limited amount of benefit in the retelling of marvelous personal experiences that happened to any of us, since they cannot be proved to anyone but ourselves. And there is no benefit at all in wallowing around in endless and useless debates about the christ Jesus versus the man Jesus, or Moses, Mohammed or anyone else some people call visionary. Therefore, let us defend those with a different point of view than ours with a loving answer from the next age, for the spirit is given to us all and shows us a much greater defense of different beliefs and practices being right and proper. This undeniable truth is: Everyone ruled by love has salvation.

Surely this is clear. The oak tree would be a fool to scoff at the pine tree so very different. Both trees are magnificent in their own ways, and it is the same way with people, for it just does not matter what religion, if any, people ascribe to. If they are ruled by love, then they are a friend. And time will prove all the different perspectives from those of us ruled by love as worthy of having been heard. The spirit is poured out on the whole world, meaning we all have access to the same information, and we will all interpret and be moved by it differently.

Why care if a loving person believes different things than us? The opinion of such a person is just as good as ours, even if it is not for our heart. Again, just as there are many great trees of different types in the forest, there are many great people of different beliefs in the world. The only thing that matters is if they are ruled by love. Anyone who submits to this highest authority is worth our friendship.

The disregard for love as the only real authority is precisely the problem when it comes to religions of the world. We should not ever let anyone dictate to us what to do or think when it comes to spiritual matters. By its very nature true religion is personal, and therefore cannot be dictated to others.

People sometimes get inspired about the mysteries of life and will share their personal philosophies about it. They may even prophecy or endeavor to speak for "god" after becoming overwhelmed by other spirits and their own egos. Such behavior is largely delusional and any prophesy stemming from it is rightly utterly false to most people, yet the words will in fact be inspiration and truth to someone.

Other people are better able to control their egos and may talk about their philosophy/spirituality to others, or they may write things down, or someone else may write what they heard. Though the proponents of philosophical/spiritual things, myself included, may believe every word they speak to be true, in all of these cases it is still opinion. And we all need to treat these things as such. Think for yourself!

Every religion has at first reflected the personality and motivations of its organizers. Then it slowly gets reinterpreted in small to large part to reflect the personality and motivations of the people who inherit its custodianship. The Christian Bible contains a myriad of mistakes, tamperings, and outright fabrications. It was this way from the start, before anything was written down and it was all verbal, and the fiction only got worse for centuries afterwards. It is not the "unquestionable word of God" as those ministers who practice priestcraft sell it, and though bits and pieces are inspired, the vast majority of the Bible is not. The cornerstone of all life – love one another – is in its pages, and with this one giant pearl, everything that has been added or twisted by the arrogant or business-minded has been given the benefit of the doubt, unless you really take time to think it through.

Except for love, thinking is the best of all the gifts from God. But thinking leads to questions, and questions are something most religious leaders do not like. This is because so much of what religions entail cannot withstand the scrutiny. But think you must.

Though I cannot prove it to anyone but myself, the specks of wisdom scattered throughout the Bible have their origin in a small number of mostly unknown people scattered throughout antiquity. These people had a profound grasp of spiritual things, both revealed and realized, and they shared what they understood as best they could. Some who heard were so moved by what they received that they in turn told it to others, and so on, and so forth (occasionally misinterpreting things in the retelling). More often though, others were misled by dreams or visions, while still others, filled with jealousy or seeking attention, fabricated their own inspirations, as even greater numbers of people perverted the universal truth about love into a business for money and influence, adding more fiction for their own selfish purposes.

The Christian religion, like Judaism, Islam, and all the others make no sense for spiritual adults. This is because each of us is an individual and the spirit of love is fully available to us all, forever. If our interactions with other people are ruled by love for them, the only conclusion about religion is that it must be entirely personal. Those ruled by love can never insist that someone else believe what they do, even if that other soul may appear to be hopelessly lost. To do so is a conceit equal to presuming to be able to speak for the combined spirit of the very Eternal itself.

Compared to love, no religion ever has, or ever will matter – except to the spiritually dead!

Although the checkered and painful future of mankind in this age will be one of slow growth, eventually we will be one united species. More religious lies, persecutions, terrorisms and wars are yet to be, but they will pass. The distant future will see us crossing space to visit the planets of other stars as easily as we cross oceans today. Present day religions will have long since perished, all of us knowing clearly that we report directly to the spirit of love that dwells within us. No persons among us will be so arrogant as to put themselves between another and their god.

If we could talk to leaves of a tree and ask them what they see, each would answer differently. Those in close proximity would answer similarly, while those on opposite sides of the tree might answer profoundly differently. It is just the same with people whose experiences and background are similar or different.

But if you asked each leaf the view they see looking through the stem where they connect to the tree, then the answer would be identical. Conversely, among people, love is our universal view, the identical stem we all connect to life by, and looking through the eyes of love enables us to accept and sometimes even understand differing points of view. Humanity is a big forest with room for many kinds of trees, and for this we should all be grateful, for life would be eternal hell indeed if we were all the same.

World peace begins person to person.

Love one another.

Life Story

A small child stares into a lonely sky,
And asks himself his first, "Who am I?"
He feels something missing and struggles to know,
"Why are things so empty?" and, "Into what do we grow?"

The first words of sense was a comment by Christ,
About "love one another," and I knew it was right.
But selfish and stupid I went my own way,
And challenged the spirit to "Prove what you say."

If love is the answer, our friend, that you claim,
I'll test it by leaving, though I know it won't change.
I'll do what I want and hardly listen at all,
Because I know it must catch me when I start to fall.

Such was my thinking when I chose to try sin,
I denied what was certain, I just wouldn't give in.
Sorry, my friend, about love you were right,
And though I was a fool you gave up your life.

But now I know better, and I'll do what you say,
Only wishing I'd come sooner to follow the way.
But here's where I found it, so here I will stand,
And I promise to share it whenever I can.

- 1985

The years went on by and my faith was true,
But my prayers went unanswered, by me and by you.
Son of god, son of man, this is what you are,
But thank you for showing me the sins in my star.

I still keep my promise to "love one another,"
And I'll always love you, son of man, younger brother.
Thanks for your help, ours sins are forgiven,
But enough of religion, it's time to start living.

Does my faith make you angry? I get no reply.
Did you hope I would fail and then watch me die?
Your silence, you hoped, it would count as a try,
But your lack of response, it revealed your lies.

I kept my promise to you. Did you think that I wouldn't?
So where is my comfort? You refuse though you shouldn't.
You must be jealous I'm faithful, so your anger stays,
Well, my friend, I still love you, but please go away.

How can I say this, after all you have done?
Have you forgot Jacob, who wrestled – near won?
And what was his reward for perseverance so true?
You crippled him for life, then wanted "thank you."

And what about Job? About him you proclaimed:
"Not one is more righteous." His reward was more pain!
So sometimes, we see, you forget right from wrong,
And like them, I'm a draw, or our fight will go on.

I have nothing left to lose... Okay, I never had more,
But my wife was mistaken when she ended with war.
For my heart was speaking: "Wait, I will take her."
But she was like me, lost in self-righteous anger.

Do you get it, my friend? Can't you see I still cry?
You mock me and challenge: Do I understand why?
Yes, you hung on a cross, but that's nothing new.
Selfish young woman, this fool still loves you.

- 1989

More years went by and our faith was still true,
Our childhood hopes, they keep shining through.
The reflection in the mirror, we brought it to life,
It has a mind of its own, and it too is right.

We're identical and opposite, perfect yet sometimes wrong,
We rejoice to discover our love will always go on.
In the face of infinity, "Who am I?" was unknown.
I would have died without you, to end my alone.

They were right, love wins, its echo we are.
In me is your origin, same for me in your star.
A miracle, some call it, or the power above,
Life forever inside us, because we believe love.

Some say death ends the bond, take another, get back in it,
But if love lives forever, reunion takes but a minute.
For those children, as such, see much smaller spaces,
True friends love forever, no one takes their places.

So I continue to wait, though demons oppose,
I don't care what they say, I know what I know.
Older sister, younger brother, Janet Lynn, beloved wife,
Heart and soul, spiritual twin, the christ light of my life.

- 2004

Notes

Denominations
1. 1 Corinthians 1:12-13, 3:4

Women Ministers
1. 1 Corinthians 14:34-36
2. Judges 4:4-6
3. Luke 2:36-38

Holy Days
1. Galatians 3:2-3
2. Jeremiah 31:31-33
3. Matthew 12:40
4. Mark 14:2
5. Luke 22:8
6. John 19:31, 42
7. Luke 24:44

We Are Gods
1. John 10:34
2. Psalms 82:6
3. Hebrews 12:9

Marriage in Heaven
1. Matthew 25:1
2. Song of Solomon 3:11

Eternal Hell
1. Luke 16:26
2. Revelation 21:7

The Trinity
1. Psalms 110:1
2. Zechariah 12:8
3. John 12:28

A God Grows Up
1. Psalms 2:7

Mistakes
1. Isaiah 50:1
2. Zechariah 13:6

Judas
1. Isaiah 42:19
2. Psalms 22:1-6
3. 2 Samuel 11:2-17
4. Psalms 139:22-24

Prophecy
1. Zechariah 13:3

Different Realities
1. Luke 17:37

Equality and the Sexes
1. Revelation 12:1
2. Mark 9:48
3. Jeremiah 30:6

Inexorable Conclusions
1. John 16:12-13

Selfish Young Man – Part II

Contents of Selfish Young Man - Part II

Introduction

Additional Commentaries

- Metamorphosis
- Additions
- Spiritual Damage
- Suicide
- Homosexuality
- Anti-Christ
- Atheism
- Religion

Poems

- Ancestors
- Fearless
- Infinity
- Sun of God

Introduction to Selfish Young Man - Part II

At the beginning of life our elders provide us everything and we give nothing in return. And though we slowly learn to give, by the time of puberty we are the very definition of selfishness and self-righteousness. In other words, we truly are a satan. But it does make sense, for if we are going to live forever, then how wise can we really be at the beginning of our life. We are next to nothing compared to eternity.

As we grow from childhood to adulthood we begin contemplating the mysteries of life and an endless number of questions start coming to mind about our existence. Knowing that it is human nature to seek to discover ourselves, some people make a business of it. Hence we have religions.

As for the Christian religions, Jesus was enlightened but many words have been put in his mouth by the people who turned him into a business, for they realized if they put Jesus above us, then they could be above us in his absence.

The practitioners of priestcraft, god businessmen, know that confidence sells, so they deliver their messages as if their every opinion, delusion or lie was a fact. And to help sell it, they talk of loving each other, the universal truth that no one can deny, all the while pretending to have special access to a truth that we all have innately.

But aside from what may or may not be true, and this is very important, there is a profound difference between what a person knows and what a person believes. Most people confuse what they believe as what they know.

Everyone has access to the spirit of God, which communicates with us at the highest level each of us is able to understand, always guided by its endless love, so no intermediaries stand between you and your God. Words like "love one another" carry with them their own authority. But with this one great pearl of wisdom, the man-made words of God annexed to this knowledge are often given too much credit.

The inspirations of Moses, Jesus, and Mohammed were all warped into businesses, leading to Judaism, Christianity and Islam. All of these religions have inflicted monumental suffering from their fanaticism. They would not have done so if they were truly ruled by love.

Look at Gandhi to see how an imperfect man can still be enlightened and effect great changes. If it were not for modern technology recording some of the things he did, then business minded Indians would right now be warping his legacy into Gandhianity for money and power, and within a few centuries his feet of clay would be forgotten.

My books are about what I know: That we should love one another. My books are also about what I believe, which is almost everything else I ever wrote. I ask the reader to think about what I have to say, then agree to disagree with me wherever we do, subject to love, because of love.

Regardless of the many things that different people believe, everyone ruled by love has eternal life. I also know this.

David Allan

Additional Commentaries

Metamorphosis

What if the many different parts of our bodies were all so in harmony with each other that the attributes and skills of every one of them were available to any other member?

In this scenario, we could ask our feet to look at something with our eyes. The strength of our legs would be at our fingertips if needed. Our hair or fingernails, having no pain sensors in them, could absorb a wound of any magnitude and we would not feel any hurt.

These unusual combinations are an effort to describe what complete sharing in the spiritual realm would be like, for imagine what kind of abilities you would have if you could share in all the attributes that others possess. For those of us ruled by love, this is just a fraction of the kind of metamorphosis that is coming for us in the next age.

In short, with harmony and goodwill in union with all the other spirits ruled by love, our every good imagination becomes real and our every bad thought is gently corrected by our new family of friends.

Love begins our omnipotence, omnipresence, and eternal life.

Most important, it begins true happiness.

Additions

When I married my wife I wanted her to be my foremost friend forever. I still feel that way and believe I always will. Therefore, she could tell any other woman that she was above all of them, and it would be true, but only as it applies to me. She could also say that no other woman can come to me except by her, for no woman who rejects her as my foremost would be welcomed by me. Conversely, no other man can come to her except by me, meaning, accepting that I was her first true love and that she will always love me.

In the physical realm, we both gave our virginity away without much thought, reckless adolescents that we were. And while we may have liked the person we gave it to, we did not love them as a soul mate.

But spiritually speaking, our virginity is another matter. My wife and I have given this to each other, by definition, since we came to life due to each other's love and suffering more than anyone else among our peers.

In other words, no one will ever take our places with each other. Real love makes additions, not substitutions.

The question is not whether we can love more than one person an infinite amount, (of course we can). But when it comes to adding soul mates, the heart must be right in the matter, understanding that a loved one is never really gone, but simply absent until another day and age. This is one reason why many widowed people never remarry.

Forever is the only amount of time long enough to be friends for those who truly love each other.

Spiritual Damage

Humans are both visible and invisible, meaning we have a physical existence and a spiritual presence as well. Our spiritual self is eternal, but our physical manifestation is only temporary, the essence of its original substance resulting from true give touching receive, and in so doing bringing both exponentially more life.

Everywhere we look, the temporary visible physical world teaches us about eternal invisible things. There are many invisible universal constants, all of which are spiritual in nature, and the ones that last forever are all aspects of love.

In the temporary physical world, permanent, lifelong damage can occur. One obvious example is how some people have lost limbs, and while the person still exists in the flesh there is permanent damage. Or perhaps a tree is hit by lightning, or damaged in the wind.

In the same way, spiritual injuries can occur. And just like the loss of a limb, spiritual wounds sometimes last a lifetime. But this is where the spiritual is temporary, for even though the injuries can be so horrific that some people lose their sanity, (a physical representation of spiritually dying), just like some physical deaths are brought back to life, so it is in these cases. And the spirit of love never gives up trying to heal spiritual injuries, spanning multiple ages and dimensions as needed, forever committed, it will always be there for anyone who turns to look for it.

Even mere depression indicates some spiritual wound or missing attribute of love. And this is why love is so important, for things like forgiveness, tolerance, kindness and courage, to name just a few of the aspects of love, can go a very long way in healing spiritual suffering. For when the mentally wounded or broken are loved, they can sometimes take hold of that kindness received to heal whatever is injured.

We see in ourselves how all of the fruits of the spirit of love work together to help us, which in turn sets an example for us to follow.

Suicide

Society's blanket condemnation of suicide is indicative of mankind's overall fear of death. However, suicide is understandable sometimes, usually in the case of great feelings of guilt, hopelessness, pain, or sorrow.

Such a thing is obviously not to be taken lightly, but not from fear of incurring wrath or punishment for such an act, which are opinions from people so frightened of death that they cannot envision ending their own life under any circumstances. The fact is that suicide is sometimes quite brave. Heroic stories of people embracing certain death to save someone else's life are legendary. But stop and think it over if the reason is not that noble.

Yes, it is your life, so you may do whatever you want with it. And there may be good reasons, as you see it, that aren't as obvious as the self-sacrifice I just cited. But even if you believe you can justify ending your own life in the spirit of love, noting how moons do eclipse planets sometimes, remember how rarely eclipses happen and how brief they always are. Be sure you are not trying to enter the spiritual realm before you are ready – before you are invited. Many premature births are stillborn or die soon after, while many more are handicapped. And all of them need extra care at first. You can be sure these same dangers apply when spiritual birth is self-induced without a pure cause.

So, if you are broken hearted to the point of despair, I urge you, please hold on for every speck of spiritual growth that you can before your birth into the next age. It will most certainly happen in due time, just like a pregnancy results in childbirth, when the time is right.

The great spirit of love, that we are all connected to, should always be our guide, even in the worst of times.

Homosexuality

The cause of homosexuality is always something missing spiritually.

For example, homosexuality can be an angry choice, resulting from the anger left over from when we tore apart from one body in to two, which was caused by our selfishness. I think that is the most common reason. But it may also be the result of beloveds trying to share each other's temples and falling short due to fear, or doubt, or conceit.

Consider that Jesus called mankind the "sons of women" but referred to himself as the "son of man."

The meanings of these words are difficult for many people, and my opinions here are probably more controversial than anything else I ever wrote, generating hatred from pharisees for all kinds of reasons. Still, it remains that one conclusion about Jesus calling himself the son of man while calling the rest of us the sons of women is simply this: Jesus was formerly a female in another dimension and wanted to know, from the heart, what it would be like to be a male. Therefore, his beloved spiritual twin (Melchizedek) granted it, and Jesus lived an additional life as a man. This happened while Melchizedek, formerly a male, lived an additional life as a woman, granted by Jesus. This is one of the things that was meant in the scripture, "frail woman becomes manly" and also by the passage in the book of Revelations that pictures Jacob as a woman with the moon as her footstool. This also ties in with different realities existing in the same place and at the same time.

What this all symbolizes is the equality between give and receive, the two faces of love, finally taken to heart by a satan, the morning star who dawned into sunrise, to use the metaphors from the Bible.

True give, gives completely, even the ability to give is given.

Or put another way, a spirit that was completely self-centered, receive only, spiritually speaking, not only embraced give, but then elevated this highest principle of love above its own self.

So Jesus was not a homosexual. He really accepted this gift of knowledge from his beloved Melchizedek and lived an entire lifetime as a heterosexual male. In fact, it is quite likely Jesus was married and had children.

If these explanations do not set with you, ask yourself this question: Do you love your husband or wife enough to share the essence of who and what you are?

If you really love your spouse, you would have to answer yes if they asked you to share your unique gender perspective.

Through the power of the great spirit of love, these kinds of things can and do happen.

But what if a husband and wife attempt such a thing but then partially reject it due to fear, or doubt, or conceit, and therefore do not truly take it to heart?

Is this a thing to be persecuted? Certainly not. This failure to give or receive completely, as the case may be, is no worse, spiritually speaking, than a baby falling while trying to learn to walk. You would not curse a baby for stumbling, would you? Or course not.

But homosexuality is a dead end, always failing to deliver spiritual fulfillment. The two faces of love, give and receive, represented by male and female, are both required to be complete. If your union is give-give, or receive-receive, you are by definition lacking half a spiritual dimension. An excellent physical example is seen in the way magnets of the same attraction do not stay joined to each other unless forced.

So homosexuality is immature and does not bear fruit, spiritually speaking, but it is not a crime as some in the priestcraft portray it.

Anti-Christ

The priestcraft makes a big fuss about anything "anti-christ", warning followers to avoid questioning the authority of the christ Jesus.

But this is just a clever business tactic, like the concept of eternal hell, for dogmas like these suspend logical thinking by frightening the listener. It is very difficult to consider different opinions when you have been brainwashed into fearing that examining church doctrines will lead to death.

Religions are rightfully afraid of losing their power and influence if people truly think for themselves, for honest reflection realizes that the authority of love is an innate knowledge that stands on its own and carries its own authority. People would then rightly reject anyone who dared speak for god, since the spirit of love is already within them. Every so-called word of god that has ever been spoken was man-made, even the wise words, and as such, have no authority over one's inner soul, for no person is above another in the spiritual realm.

A person may speak to the spirit of god, and a person may speak about god, but no person may speak for god, except to themselves.

Honest reflection also brings us to the realization that we are all "christs," because we have all suffered unjustly at the hand of others.

No matter how hopelessly lost some other soul may seem to be, we cannot ever speak as god to them. The reverse situation applies, too, as some souls become so attuned to the universal truth of love that it might seem like a god, or his representative, was speaking. But even if the advice or message is true, it is not the voice of god.

As the christ Gandhi said, "An eye for an eye leaves the whole world blind." This is a great example of the wisdom of forgiveness. And when you forgive others their trespasses, like the christ Jesus did, then you have truly transcended into another dimension of life.

Atheism

The reason we cannot understand our spiritual parents clearly is exactly the same principle as if a baby in the physical womb tried to envision his mother and father's appearance. An accurate description would fail miserably for the fetus, but it could eventually arrive at the correct conclusion that something is on the outside of its tiny world within the womb.

Our own current reality shows us how much profoundly greater the next life is by comparison. This can be seen by looking backwards or forwards, trying to understand the past or envision the future. This is much the same as if butterflies and caterpillars were to contemplate each other. But the caterpillar knows much less than the butterfly, just like an acorn understands almost nothing compared to the oak, or an infant compared to its parents.

No matter what we say about whether there is a god, or not, there is always someone or something that physically preceded us, and this applies spiritually as well.

In the physical world we call our progenitors by the word "parents," and the word fits well in the spiritual sense, too. For the eternal highest authority, namely love, in every case was given to us before we ever gave any love back to anyone or anything.

As we examine our physical universe we come to realize that everything is just machinery of one sort or another. And our bodies are just organic machines. But the spiritual universe, where love reigns supreme, over all other emotions and even reason itself, is why we are more than mere machinery, more than logical conclusions. For love defies selfishness and is the universal denominator of life and eternity both, the connection between all humans, and ultimately, all forms of life, even infinity itself.

So great is the power of love, it even tolerates inferior selfish philosophies to grow until their dead end, at love's expense, and then it offers equality to those same persecutors as soon as they repent of their selfishness.

Because of this ultimate power of love, I agree when some people say there is no god, for ultimately, only love can be god.

But assuming, for the sake of discussion, that humanity was just an accident or random chance, the fact remains that each of us began life by receiving. In every case, someone, or something, gave to us first. This physical fact is representative of spiritual fact.

In the physical sense, we begin by receiving air, then milk, but in the spiritual sense we "take" before we ever "give" to anyone. Many years later, hopefully the principles of love awaken within us and we turn around to seek a way to make up for our selfishness. But the point is we begin by receiving. Physically, someone or something gave to us first, and spiritually, we took from someone without their willing participation. And in the spiritual sense, the origin of give is actually the principle itself, since give is the fullest flower of love.

Therefore, even though the principle of love is the zenith of thought, so one could argue there is no god, this is not the same thing as having no parents. Endless examples in nature show everything has an origin of some sort.

In other words, even if one believes there is no god, the fact remains we still had parents, a form of creator with god like abilities by comparison – at least at the start of our life here. And even though the principle of love is, in the final analysis, our only true parents, (with our spiritual fathers and mothers ultimately becoming just friends, like our physical parents become), the fact still remains: We all began both our physical and spiritual life by receiving. And this is humbling, since eternal life begins with giving.

So atheism makes interesting points, but so does deism, which correctly looks to higher life forms than puny mortal man. The result is that true religion has but one universal precept, which is love and its many attributes. And this spirit of love is the only thing each of us must obey, utterly independent from anything contradictory to its absolute authority over everything.

Religions

Could an acorn describe what it is like to be an oak tree?

Though it obviously would have some faint idea what it would be like, having originated from the tree, any great understanding would not be possible. This is just the same as how a caterpillar could not understand much about its next life, but having originated from a butterfly, it knows enough to lie down and sleep in confidence of a glorious awakening.

In other words, the inability to clearly envision our future state does not mean that we cannot know a greater age is coming, and that we will carry the life sustaining force of love with us when we cross over.

Since these kinds of spiritual things are an innate knowledge, yet difficult to describe with words by adults, and impossible for children to explain, clever individuals have always used spiritual awareness for profit and power.

But, whenever some conceited soul pretends they know god best, people eventually suffer for it.

If god is love, we do not need religions. Furthermore, if god is love, and love and money together is prostitution, then what is religion but spiritual harlotry perfected into a science.

Even if we merely try to describe "god" the result must necessarily emphasize the motivations and attributes of the person doing the describing. In the best of situations this over-emphasizes some spiritual talents of love while downplaying others. It misinforms and outright lies in the worst cases.

A group effort to describe what god is like yields barely better results, for it excludes something from every individual in the compromise, therefore resulting in some level of dissatisfaction for all. Put another way, everyone always disagrees with some part of a group description of what is god. And this is perfectly right, because we are all individuals and therefore different by definition. It is not possible to be the exact same as anyone else for it would mean the loss of our individuality, our identity itself, thereby destroying the "I am" in each us.

We are all individuals, so true religion, which represents the very essence of our innermost self, must also be individual, and therefore always completely independent. No one has ever agreed with everything someone else believed. And no one ever will. This alone makes adherence to any religion an error.

Stop and think about Moses, the magician who wrote an entire religion for a people. To sell it, he informed them that they were god's chosen people, that is to say, god's favorite. And they, in turn, announced it to their neighbors with a sword. Then they compounded their crime by citing the rejection of their claim of superiority as proof of the inferiority of their victims. This is wicked conceit to the point of madness.

The heart of all religious fanaticism always hides self-righteousness, the essence of which can be summed up by saying: "I am better than you." Then it gets worse, for the next downward step says in its heart: "The fact you do not see I am better than you proves that I am!"

But the arrogance of the Israelites is nothing new. We only need to look at the Egyptians that preceded them or the Christians and Muslims that followed, to see that god businesses keep evolving. But the one constant is that the priestcraft cleverly stroke the egos of the stupid and arrogant with the same old message: "We are better than others." And the reasons why we are better are always things that imply "we are more loving" and "god loves us more."

Religions are the worst diseases in human history and are in fact the spiritual equivalent of a contagious illness. And putting the precepts of any religion above "love one another" is the spiritual equivalent of being terminally ill.

Compared to love, no religion has ever mattered, or ever will, except to the spiritually dead!

Poems

Ancestors

Take a journey with our minds and time travel to the past,
With our power of reason we see the way it was quite fast,
The truth is prehistoric man was smarter than we know,
This logical conclusion is not too hard to show.
Think about the daily grind of hunt and gather clans,
Survival was a struggle, made a living with their hands,
But depending on the season many hours are at night,
So even after sleeping they were up without daylight.
Large groups awake in darkness, how do you pass the time?
Huddled 'round a campfire, whole families shared their minds.
They talked for hours every night, things plain to paranormal,
All their knowledge passed like this, the learning was phenomenal.
It's wrong to underestimate their thoughtful state of mind,
Philosophy was love and nature, it's we who are behind.
The ancients saw, caterpillars crawl, knew one day they would fly.
They saw acorns vanish, up came oaks, somehow they didn't die.
Now we have religions, and though different in every nation,
They cannot hide any of God's original information.
So think about true religion, in nature, not institutions,
God is free, God is love, love with money is prostitution.

Fearless

CONSIDER THE FOLLOWING...

Two physical seeds.......... One spiritual seed.
Conceived your body....... Conceiving your soul.
Earth now........................ Afterlife soon.
Born in the flesh............... Birth in the spirit.
Discarded placenta........... Discard body.
Blood............................... Love.
Temporary....................... Permanent.
Life force......................... Life flow.
Entered crying.................. Enter laughing.
Miss this world? .... Did you miss your placenta?

PICTURE IT THIS WAY...

FIRST...
One physical seed (sperm) and one physical seed (egg),
In blood conceived your life on earth,
Born crying into temporary life of flesh,
The placenta obsolete.

THEN....
One spiritual seed (love) and one physical seed (body),
In love conceives your life in the universe,
Born laughing into permanent life of spirit,
The body obsolete.

LOVE CONQUERS DEATH!

Infinity

Some people think that their physical uniqueness,
Means the opposite gender has spiritual weakness,
But men and women can't be the other's superior,
Different, is all, which does not mean inferior.
Look at the evidence, there's only one conclusion,
For we were all created to need the same solution.

Every pair of twin members, that we can think to name,
Are basically like equals, reflections of the same,
Your arms and your shoulders, just like your legs and feet,
Twins joined in one body, and the middle's where they meet.
See how in between those pairs, sit all the single members,
And they are always placed midway, in or near the center,
No matter where you look, head or heart, and yes the soul,
The singles always link the pairs, make one amazing whole.

Now think about your best friend, regard their special build,
They have parts that represent a soul that's not fulfilled,
For each of us is half complete, designed from up above,
Give and receive, boy and girl, the two sides of perfect love.
Each holds missing parts, we cannot live without each other,
Two wrap into one, we clothe ourselves with one another.

Picture now, the union grows, physical into spiritual,
If minds meld like a climax, we really could do miracles.
Once we linked like this, we'd share everything together,
But also independent, the design a joy forever.
"I am" is where we start, the essence of original thought,
But the answer to "What am I", is the first thing we are taught.
The never-changing, ever-changing answer that I see,
Begins when "What am I" is simply answered by "We",
For it requires eternal friends for our souls to be free,
So love starts one plus one, which starts Infinity.

Sun of God

Earth thought the Sun revolved around him,
Moon thought the Earth revolved around her,
Man and woman are rebuked.

Both tried to be – The God...
Instead of – a god.

But a parole from celestial prisons is possible,
Granted by love,
If they get off their pedestal and throne,
Serve others instead,
Embrace love.

True give, gives completely, even give is given,
Receive returns it multiplied,
Two unique entities permanently bind,
One new being.
Yet still two.
An explosion of light,
Showers new life into infinity.
They awake with the power of the Sun,
Equals.
Free.
No law but love.
Stars are born.
We are gods.

Wiser Old Man

Contents of Wiser Old Man

Introduction to Wiser Old Man

Three or four years old is the youngest age I can recall inquiring about my existence. By the time I was five my questions were frequent, but the only thing I could understand with certainty was that we should love each other, and that I was going to die someday. At six years old I was positive that much higher life forms than humans existed, but I still understood almost nothing about who, and what, we are.

Of course, my questioning usually met with answers that resulted in me asking more questions, and I recall with fondness how my parents would often have to resort to answering with that most common of childhood answers: "You'll understand when you're older."

It was about this time that I first heard about Jesus from an acquaintance of the family, who said his paramount teaching was that we should love each other. I was curious to know more. In the next five years I would hear more stories about Jesus, many of which seemed like fairy tales, yet the fact remained he said we should love each other, and treat others as we would like to be treated. I knew that was absolutely true.

As for school education, at thirteen years old that was cut short by an overwhelming desire to be outside of the traditional classroom. It had become agony for me, so I didn't participate much after seventh grade, virtually stopped attending after eighth grade, and officially dropped out when I was 16 years old. I would later enroll in night school to earn a high school diploma, while I worked during the day, and even attended college for a year, where I again lost interest in school and majored in cutting classes.

My employment history begins at fourteen with a series of menial jobs over the next 10 years. Most of these positions I excelled at, but disdained for the low pay, the effect on my self-esteem, and the dissatisfaction that lack of challenge brings. But one very good thing happened during that period – I met my beloved Jan the winter after I turned twenty one. We were immediately inseparable.

Nearing my twenty-third birthday I became interested in learning more about Jesus so I read the Bible cover to cover. I found it to be encouraging, even enlightening, since despite its patchwork writing, I saw its conclusion was that love is above all things. However, the fact remained that much of it didn't make sense, and so it was after this that I decided to enroll in seminary school to learn from experts. What a waste of time that turned out to be – I quit after my first day as they had nothing to offer. Without laboring over the details, the place felt strange, almost lifeless. Years later, I realized this was because religions are businesses and many of those people were there to hone their priestcraft. They were looking for power and profit. I was looking for answers.

(To digress a moment on a tactic religions often deceive with: They talk of having faith. This is excellent when it means we should trust in love. But when having faith is a directive that tells us to say we understand something, because we think someday we will understand, then that is lying. Even worse, one is then in the precarious position of being unable to explain their beliefs rationally, which requires more lies or delusions to defend them.)

So I escaped from pharisees, yet the fact remains we should love each other, and Jesus was the person I most associated with that idea. But at this point I had no further interest in studying.

Another year went by, Jan and I eloped, but my inability to find decent employment was demoralizing as my income was incapable of ever supporting a family. After that, another two years of near poverty went by, so in desperation I asked god to have mercy and help me. Soon after, I found a good job.

Just two years later Jan and I had a son, and I was in the midst of an excellent career with a computer equipment wholesaler. Having been promoted several times, I was now branch manager for the Mid-Atlantic region, based in Philadelphia, where the company had relocated us. Then, as my twenty-ninth birthday approached, a storm was brewing... First, the company's managers had become rivals instead of teammates, while the job itself had become routine and was no longer fulfilling. Worse than that, my wife and I were terribly homesick, plus she had been ill for months and doctors could not figure out what the problem was. So I resigned my position and the three of us moved back to the Chicago suburbs to be near our families... And then the lightning struck – my wife was diagnosed with cancer. Thus I began caring for our one and a half year old son while my wife was constantly in the hospital undergoing chemotherapy treatments for the next eight months.

During this time I immersed myself in the second serious Bible study of my life, this time reading it over and over, perhaps ten hours a day on average, for the next seven months. I even attended church for a short time, though it always felt like something was wrong about the place, so I stopped going. I only ended my full time studies because I was broke and had to return to work, putting our son in a daycare center each morning and picking him up in the evening. My wife died a month later.

What a heartbreak. I didn't want her to die, but she did, and I was about to discover the hardest lesson of my life – that I had been like a satan. Too heartbroken to function normally, I quit my job two months after her death and began yet another full-time Bible study. Four months after that I was going broke again and moved across country to be closer to my parents, who had themselves recently relocated to the suburbs of Washington, DC for employment.

My days for the next year consisted of little but caring for my son and taking long, soul-searching drives in the country. I didn't work a single day or read a single verse.

As it happened, my parents were unhappy with their employment and the rat race of city life, so they decided to go into business for themselves and asked me to join them. Soon we all relocated to a rural community and started a business that lasted over 30 years (though only my parents were involved start to finish, as I soon went on to other things).

So I rented my own place again and set about to rebuild my life. But I was still too heartbroken to function well, so two and a half years after my wife had died, I quit work, moved with my son to much cheaper quarters, and immersed myself in another marathon of full time Bible studies. For over two years I again spent about 10 hours a day reading the Bible. And that was all I did, except for spending time with my little boy, (who is now a grown man and continues to be the greatest joy remaining in my life). When my savings were exhausted I occasionally sold belongings to pay bills, even my bedroom set and then my car, as my little boy and I were reduced to poverty and walking for the last year of this period.

It was towards the end of this time, in 1989, that I wrote the nucleus of what would become my first book, which I put away so my son could read it in the future. (My full time study of the Bible ended after that and I went back to regular life again, first doing construction work and then selling boats. After that I started selling real estate, became a broker, and eventually opened my own successful realty company. Today, I'm elderly and collecting my retirement benefits.) However, I did continue to study and write intermittently after 1989, spending thousands of hours on additional study, plus thousands more hours in reflection and writing, eventually expanding my work to three times its original length.

In 2004 I published my expanded collection of essays as a book titled *Selfish Young Man*. Since then I have not studied the scriptures at all, never will again, and no longer even own a Bible. However, I did still write intermittently and several years after the first publication I put together another group of essays titled *Selfish Young Man - Part II*.

Having devoted a huge amount of my life to the study of Christian scripture and natural philosophy, I think my opinions can provoke a little thinking for most readers. Note that I am well aware there are few ideas of which we can be absolutely sure about, but some things carry their own authority, such as trying to love each other and following the golden rule. The bottom line is you can think for yourself, so as I have said previously about my writing: Read it, get out of it what you can, leave the rest behind.

Lastly, please overlook any grammatical errors, for writing was never my profession, or even much of an ability until later in life. Also, my beliefs and opinions on several topics expressed herein are a little different now than they were years ago. Change for everyone goes on forever, and for this reason I have not rewritten things from long ago to better explain my present beliefs, nor have I spent much time polishing more recently published pieces. They communicate well enough. The important thing is to promote love instead of religion, encourage independent thinking, share ideas, and provide a little cheer.

Poems

Aesop Would Be Pleased

This is a fable, yet the truest of stories,
And yes, there's a moral to this allegory.
Students in Athens had thought for a while,
Who is the prettiest in all the Greek Isles?

For thousands of years, the winner, of course,
Helen of Troy, launched the ships and the horse.
All throughout Greece, her likeness abounds,
Statues and busts in the squares of all towns.

But who is it now, with these centuries passed?
And so a great plan was conceived and then hatched.
Thousands of photos of common Greek women,
Were merged, morphed, and blended into a vision.

Computers then averaged this data divine,
Every possible feature, except for the mind.
Eyes, nose and lips, forehead and chin,
There wasn't a feature that wasn't put in.

Now here is a shock you will surely enjoy,
The composited picture was Helen of Troy!
Even Plato might think that answer was scary,
The prettiest woman was most ordinary!

Mr. Slippery

Washington and Jefferson would never have believed,
How selfish are the leaders of the nation they conceived,
Things are so corrupt you know that even God is grieved.

Tell us Mr. Slippery, what are your key positions?
Then they double talk and talk, they're always on a mission,
If caught in lies, no problem, it wasn't their decision.

Swiss banking on their payoffs, deposited in laughter,
They fleece the lamb electorate, or lead us to the slaughter,
Then after screwing us, it's girls younger than their daughters.

Fake smiles always beaming, speeches full of banality,
These professional actors with defective morality,
Break hearts with broke promises to care for humanity.

It's all about wine, women, song, and free travels,
Sell power, free pussy, and buy judge's gavels,
While politics parties, our country unravels.

No wonder the public is sick of their actions,
For the picture is clear on these fat cat factions,
Their heads are stuck solid in anal impaction.

It's long overdue for lottery elections,
Every citizen gets a chance at selection,
Then winners might care for our country's direction.

How can these dogs ever look in a mirror?
We know the positions they hold the most dear,
Secretaries on top and voters in the rear!

World's Oldest Profession

You've heard some funny stories about a rabbi and a priest,
This one includes an imam and it's wild to say the least.
They called it interfaith discussion, to make it sound so wise,
But it was just God companies set out to proselytize.

"Thank you all so much for coming," was their opening remark.
"Welcome to our forum, we hope that light will fill the dark.
But first a little prayer, would you all please bow your heads,
And bend your knees to show you care that God hears what is said."

"Excuse me sir," I stood and asked, "Why perform this ritual?
"It really has no meaning as to love and what is spiritual.
All of us had parents that came from simple mortal man,
And they regard us face to face, and some call us right hands.
So why in heaven's name, would a God who loves me more,
Put me on my knees and have me talking towards the floor?"

Stunned and clearly shaken the youthful priest began to blush;
"Excuse me son, don't argue," was his answer in a rush.
"It's an honest question young man," I calmly answered back.
And please don't call me son, that's very arrogant in fact.
Now let me ask another thing, since you say Christ is God,
That means his death was suicide. Don't you think that's odd?"
By now the crowd was silent, could he explain those lies?
He stamped his foot and shouted, "I believe it. That is why!"

"But that is not an answer, not to any of my questions,
And furthermore I have for you a number of suggestions:
Stop pretending you have access to some special information,
Everyone who's ruled by love is sure to find salvation.
And isn't God just love, but love and money is prostitution?
The oldest men's professions are in religious institutions."

"Love carries its own authority as the real word of God.
Jesus didn't invent it, nor did Moses or Mohammed.

So much unwise fiction has been joined to that great pearl,
Self-righteous wicked people, seeking ways to rule the world."

"Slavery and royalty, God blessed those sad oppressions,
Colonists and terrorists, God blessed mass murder actions.
Wicked men and selfish nations, twist love to aid their lies,
Since time began, a billion killed, religions made them die."

"And it isn't just the Christians, the Jews are terrible too.
Moses said that they were best to milk conceited fools.
Arrogant people pay any price to feel above all others,
But the real god, the love inside, is free and calls us brothers."

"Then there's radical Islam, stupidity for a fact,
A billion crazy Muslims cheer when terrorists attack.
But since half the world is male, how are 72 brides arranged?
Does God castrate most Muslim men so they can be sex changed?"

"Death to you!" The imam raged, "No insult will I take!"
"Stone him," cried the rabbi! The priest yelled "Burn him at the stake!"
All hell broke loose, as chaos reigned, I sparked unholy war,
That I would get a martyr's death was clearly next in store!

But wise men rose to my defense and kept those dogs at bay,
So the salesmen of love tucked tail and simply slunk away.
For when did God forbid that people find him on their own?
And those who speak for God are those to whom God is unknown!

Haunted

Crack!
His jaw breaks,
Under the impact,
Of my fist.

Wham!
I shatter his teeth with my other fist.

Whack! Whack!
His nose gushes blood.

Over and over, I just keep smashing him.
Die you asshole!

I'm 13 years old,
Again.

Stop! Stop!
Snap out of this sick fantasy daydream…
Triggered by news of another school shooting,
Done by a child.
A tidal wave of memories drowned me for a moment,
My own childhood bullies…tears…humiliation…heartbreak.
Trauma.
So much worse than bleeding,
As I hemorrhaged love.

Decades ago,
But I still ache to recall it.

And I fear I will die with this hate.

In-Laws

Her mother added discord,
"His love is not enough."
My wife knew that it was,
Then forgot when times got tough.

My mother spoke so coldly,
"Not a thing your wife can do."
False reason to dislike her,
O mother, shame on you.

Her father called and told her,
"You're not my daughter anymore."
She told me that she loved me,
Then she walked right out the door.

My father's flaws were different,
From broken childhood tears,
Insensitive and distant,
Yet my best friend, I am sure.

But these were not the key things,
We know we're most to blame,
And when our kids get our age,
They will say of us the same.

Hurt parents put the blame elsewhere,
Their children's biggest fans,
But parents slowly come to know,
God has the better plans.

Generations

How many angels can dance on the head of a pin?

"All of them," my son answered loudly.

"As many as needed," I answered proudly.

"How many you want?" my dad smiled fondly.

Space Queen

Her girlfriends called her space queen, told me behind her back,
But I saw right away, the character that they lacked.
She said this, or she said that, whispers and silly giggles,
Bat their eyes and tell me lies, beg attention with a wiggle.

The difference wasn't even close; there's more I can explain,
It had to do with who was giving, and who was getting pain.
Smiling faces, frowning hearts, princesses of the college,
All that mirror time couldn't see that love possesses knowledge.

Chase anything that's shiny, they defined the nearly blind,
Vacancies above the neck, must have one first to lose one's mind.
Dull eyed and dumb as cattle, not a good girl in the herd,
No wonder she felt lost there, her heart felt kinder words.

Their credo in a nutshell, "Can't you see I'm so superior?"
But my girl saw it different, thought no one was inferior.
She was simply on a higher plane, pursuing things known wise,
The others lost in selfish, their philosophies drawing flies.

Some friends betrayed her even more, asked me to go astray,
Legs wide open, more than clear, simply call and have my way.
Her so-called friends, it's sickening, soliciting for a date,
I told them all "No thanks," I'm in love and you're too late.

Barking like angry dogs they spoke, real bitches is what I mean,
But I knew why they hated her, space queen was in my dreams.

Reunion

What a painful lesson,
But maybe soon it's through,
I'm so tired of living,
Without my best friend you.

Long ago began our journey,
Selfish spirits that found love,
We truly changed our actions,
They even noticed up above.

Saw our faces in each other's,
Found a soul mate long at last,
Thanked God for such a blessing,
Then forgot about it fast.

The details aren't important,
We know why we're apart:
I will change if you will,
The other one should start.

The day I finally woke up,
Is the day I watched you die,
In the hell called the years after,
More than a thousand times I cried.

My turn to follow you now,
To the very end, as such,
Like you, nothing will stop me,
For I owe you just as much.

Demons move the finish line,
Their lies keep slipping through,
But I will get the last laugh,
For they lost me to you.

Here's the truth I tell them:
Hurt you badly in our war.
I swear it friend, I miss you,
Don't want without you anymore.

Empty years have crawled by,
I live on memories crumbs,
We say, one day, Our Day,
God I wish that day would come.

There is only one rule,
That we love one another,
So I have waited all these years,
You're worth it my beloved.

Grown so much since back then,
Living by the golden rule,
No longer selfish young man,
Wiser old man conquered fool.

What I'm saying is I'm sorry,
Know you're broken hearted, too,
But nothing's come between us,
I am still in love with you.

Endless lonely heartaches,
Miss you more than anything,
But love can guide you to me,
So please, my freedom bring.

Decades now, no one to hug,
As long without a kiss,
Let me die, I miss your smile,
God help my soul dismiss.

Articles and Commentaries

Religion v. Reason

The practitioners of priestcraft teach us to get on our knees to talk to God. But consider how our physical parents love to talk with us face to face and all they want in return is our friendship. How much better would our spiritual parents treat us?

Religions claim that God told Abraham to kill his son. We put people in jail or asylums if they follow voices like that. A real God would be too good to ask such a thing. A real God would be too almighty to need to.

The Bible makes God say, "Kill all the Midianites, except keep the virgin girls for yourselves." Little girls owned as sex slaves? By the murderers of their families? This is the word of a God?

Or consider this decree: "No woman may teach a man." Aside from the obvious, that we all had mothers, should a grown man go through his entire life and learn nothing from half the world?

God's authorship of any religion collapses in absurdity if we just allow ourselves to think. And someday, just as we no longer believe Earth is the center of the universe, so it is that speaking for God will also pass away as ignorance. Until that day, religions will continue to stunt mankind's growth. Approximately seven billion people are subjected to their perversions of truth and common sense every day, and the world is mentally, emotionally and spiritually malnourished because of them.

The honest student of life finds that the spirit of love, the power of reason, and the creation itself hold so much more spiritual insight as to render any religion and its scriptures virtually useless. But the priestcrafters tenaciously hold us back to keep milking us, using the same conceited message that has always worked on the spiritually blind: "We are better than other people."

The political point? The union between elected officials and priestcrafters is greater than ever in the United States.

Almost every speech from our national leaders parrots the sanctimonious: "America is the greatest country on Earth." Was there ever a country so in love with itself? This is the same conceited drivel that priestcraft sells, all of them experts at stroking the ego. It's a sickness that turns out badly and we have the deeds to prove it.

Recall the religious crimes I noted earlier. The United States' self-righteousness is much the same. We have treated other nations as if we were a cruel God and made them grovel. Our conceit has led us to sacrifice tens of thousands of our own children, and millions of sons and daughters of other countries. And as for our intelligence? No other country is regarded as smart enough to teach us anything.

Contrast this to the wisdom of America's forefathers. In the 1700's individual religion was well respected and typical of the majority of the Colonies' leaders. And look what they accomplished: The end of royalty and the beginning of free speech! Today's leaders? They teach nothing. They risk nothing. They lead nowhere. Once America led by example; now we lead by brute force. The golden rule is that gold rules, as the unholy alliance between priest and politician turns us backwards. Both greedily aid and abet world slavery to billionaires, while the true religion, which is simply love and reason, is threatened with extinction yet again.

Mankind needs a spiritual revolution, another Age of Enlightenment. We need to get free of the mental stupor of Christianity, Judaism, Islam and every other self-righteous group that dares pretend to tell us "what God says." We already know what God says because we've always known: That we should love each other and treat each other as we would like to be treated! We were born with this awareness. The ideas are innate knowledge, carry their own authority, and come into sharper focus as we mature.

The stultifying influence of Christianity on rational thought has been fogging America's intellect for over 200 years. Historical facts are now so corrupted that our first five presidents, every one of them a Deist, are regularly believed to have been Christians. True, when America was a primitive agrarian society it was the custom of most political leaders to attend a church. But why? Because Sunday was the only day they could mingle with large groups of voters. Everyone was working the other six days. There was also some church attendance so as not to appear anti-Christian. The truth is, America's first five presidents and many others of that period merely tolerated Christianity, agreeing to disagree when opinions conflicted. They knew that love and reason were more important than their individual philosophical differences.

Mainstream media also fosters this false Christian history and some of our school books are virtually proselytizing. The internet is a help, but is also losing ground to revisionists. For example, when I first wrote this article, Wikipedia's entry on Benjamin Franklin, a staunch Deist, quoted a fictional letter wherein he chastised Thomas Paine for writing his seminal book The Age of Reason. That would have been a real miracle, since Franklin died four years before Paine wrote the book!

Take a look at how a few of our early presidents really felt about priestcraft. Most of these quotes are from letters to friends where they didn't have to guard their true feelings.

John Adams

"The priesthood have, in all ancient nations, nearly monopolized learning. And ever since the Reformation, when or where has existed a Protestant or dissenting sect who would tolerate a free inquiry? ...brutality is patiently endured, countenanced, propagated, and applauded. But touch a solemn truth in collision with a dogma of a sect, though capable of the clearest proof, and you will find you have disturbed a nest of hornets..."

"The Government of the United States of America is not, in any sense, founded on the Christian religion..." (From the Treaty of Tripoli in 1797. Signed by President Adams and ratified unanimously by the United States Senate. That's right, unanimously!)

Thomas Jefferson

"In every country and in every age, the priest has been hostile to liberty. He is always in alliance with the despot, abetting his abuses in return for protection to his own. It is easier to acquire wealth and power by this combination than by deserving them, and to effect this, they have perverted the purest religion ever preached to man (Deism) into mystery and jargon, unintelligible to all mankind, and therefore the safer engine for their purposes."

"The priests of the different religious sects... dread the advance of science as witches do the approach of daylight."

James Madison

"Religious bondage shackles and debilitates the mind and unfits it for every noble enterprise."

"What influence have ecclesiastical establishments had on society? In some instances they have been seen to erect a spiritual tyranny on the ruins of the civil authority; on many instances they have been seen upholding the thrones of political tyranny; in no instance have they been the guardians of the liberties of the people."

America's founding fathers were the creators of the Constitution and the Bill of Rights. They were Deists, not Christians. They were independent in their thinking, not subjected to other men.

Note that Lincoln was also a Deist. Taft and a few others were generally independent. It's good that they were, but it also shows the downward spiral of our character. Our first national leaders never prostituted themselves with the clergy for mutual benefit, or did so very little. Now they all pander with them.

Generations have passed since any president has had the depth and courage to reject pretending that the priestcrafters were above us. The same is true for almost the entire Congress, and the overall effect has been a severe reduction in the wisdom, intellect, and tolerance of the people. History shows how vehemently the priestcrafters opposed men like Jefferson and Lincoln, but they still won the Presidency. Today they couldn't get elected to city council.

We need great independent thinkers in the White House again. We need them in all elected offices. Religions always injure us politically because they need to protect their business interests. They do this by working against independent leaders because they need followers. This is not what we need.

The bottom line is this: Every person who rejects priestcraft in favor of love and reason becomes a much needed friend of humanity.

The New Crusades

Why is the United States occupying the Middle East?

Reasons frequently cited include oil, imperialism, warmongering, revenge and fighting terrorism. I leave it to others to debate what level of importance these factors hold. What concerns me is religion, another consideration, seldom discussed in the West, but which is a greater cause than any other, with the probable exception of how it relates to money.

The people involved in these wars are from cultures overwhelmingly influenced by Abrahamic religions. The idea that "God loves us more" is a driving force in all three. And they all have "holy" books to try to prove it. If you can pin them down on their rationale for actually believing these things, their answer is: "We are better people." This goes around in circles as it's the same self-righteousness at heart.

A quick review...

Judaism: They believe they are God's favorite. The leaders of the Mosaic religion had a history of commanding their people to slaughter entire nations, even the babies. After 1,800 years without a country of their own, they emigrated to Palestine en masse and then refused to grant a homeland to the people who were there first.

Christianity: They believe they are God's favorite. When Christian leaders came to power they plundered the entire world in the name of God. The people of every non-Christian country on Earth were slaughtered, enslaved, or treated as savages and barbarians, while colonialism destroyed the majority of their ancient cultures.

Islam: They believe they are God's favorite. Though they lag behind in civil rights, their violence is right on par. Citing the delight of God to see infidels die, which is any non-Muslim, they commit mass murders by bombing the general public. When infidels are in short supply they are happy to please the Almighty with the murders of each other.

These are the worst examples, but it demonstrates how the seeds of conceit, which these religions sow, eventually bear the fruit of crime and violence.

Imagine if someone said to you: "You are inferior to me!" This is precisely how churches, temples, and mosques are subtly training their followers to think of other people. Such conceit cannot be avoided. After all, they claim to possess the actual "Word of God." Attendees nod their heads and hearts to what the preachers are selling, and the gist of it is: "God is pleased with us" and "God is not pleased with outsiders." You hear that just being there makes you a better person than others. And if you join them (bring money) and follow obediently (stop thinking) then you're even better. People love to have their egos stroked and some will pay almost any price – body and soul – to those who do it well. Priestcraft is the oldest men's profession.

Conceit causes strife in personal life, but on an international level it's a disaster. The wars in the Middle East involve three religions that are predominant in the nations of three billion people. All of these people were exposed as children to the self-righteous doctrine that they are God's favorite. We can argue about which of these cults is the worst, but one thing is certain: The smug sense of superiority that priestcraft instilled in us during our childhood is why there is no end in sight for these new crusades. Deep down in our hearts, in this nation so historically influenced by Christians, and now also by Jews, we want the Muslims beaten and smashed. We want them dead…

In the United States these wars secretly gave most of the general public a sense of pride. Israel was nearly euphoric about them. On the surface it may not appear that way, but it doesn't take much digging to see it. Talk to almost any Christian or Jew about the wars and you can see the gleam of satisfaction. They're ashamed to admit it, but their delight becomes obvious very quickly. They just can't talk openly about what their hearts know is so morally wrong. Their dark hidden attitude is that the Muslims can go to hell.

Plain and simple, religion is the main reason we don't have a real anti-war movement. The proof of this is easily seen by remembering the public attitude against the Vietnam War. The protests had become so widespread by the time we quit, that not only were millions of people in the streets rallying against the war, but there was a multitude of churches speaking out. This is not the case with today's conflicts that are raging all over the Muslim world, but then, we never heard bad things about Buddhists when we were growing up.

These wars in the Middle East were based on reports of threats we knew were lies in the first place. And they have been spilling blood for nearly a decade with very little progress, but very substantial tears. Meanwhile, we've wasted a trillion dollars and ruined our economy. Where are the protesters? Nearly 1,000,000 people have died. Over 3,000,000 people have fled their countries. And they haven't returned home either. Do they prefer refugee camps? Almost every Iraqi citizen has dead friends or family members. The churches are silent. The temples are silent.

And it gets worse...

Not only is there no end in sight, we're expanding our attacks. In addition to wars in Iraq and Afghanistan, we are now bombing four other Muslim countries. That's war against six nations and not one of them attacked us. None of these people wanted us there. None of them want us there now. They may dislike us, but how is that God's permission to kill them? Government reports, leaked by employees with a conscience, show us that covert projects are working to destabilize almost every Muslim country in the world. Public outrage ended the Vietnam War. Private delight expands the War on Islam.

What happened to the golden rule? Christianity, Judaism and Islam all pretend to speak for God, but only one is being murdered. Behold! Christians and Jews are in complete agreement for the first time in history!

But God approves because we are better people. And God loves us more...

Keep Abortion Legal

Just as plants grow, mature, and then fade, so it is with people's bodies. The vessels our spirits dwell in are literally organic machines, for our body's growth and decline happens automatically, from start to finish, just as it does with plants.

The only part of us that is not organic machinery is our spirit, that life force which animates us and wherein each of us recognizes the "I am" of our individual essence. So the vessels we will dwell in begin at conception, but our actual spiritual life inside these machines begins when?

Surely we do not put on clothes while their fabrics are being woven, though after weaving, the cloth might possibly be cut and sewn while wearing it. Surely no one moves into a house at the start of construction, though once the foundation is in and the framework erected, then we might live there while the building is completed. So some amount of structure must come to pass before a thing can actually be used, and this same principle applies to our souls inhabiting our bodies while they are under construction in the womb.

As to the moment a soul takes up residence in a fetus, we do not know when that happens. Some might say not until the actual birth. But no one knows. Personally, I believe the moment of unity between flesh and spirit in the womb depends on the parents and the child to be, so it might be very early in the pregnancy in some cases. But it is also clear that some pregnancies are miscarried or stillborn, often when the parents truly wanted a child. So where was the unity of body and soul of the future child in those cases? It was absent is the answer. So who can truly know the moment of union? Or why it does, or does not happen?

But this we do know…

Inhaling is the first thing all newborns do or they will not live. And the last thing all of us will do in our lifetime here is exhale. This testifies to our actual physical life on Earth existing in breathing. I repeat this critical point: The first thing every person does is inhale and the last thing every person does is exhale. Our physical life here begins and ends with breathing.

Since no one can move into a home at the start of construction, and because of the facts about breathing, I believe that the union of body and soul on Earth most often begins around the time a fetus might be able to breathe on its own if born prematurely, and that a fetus is only organic machinery until such time.

Interestingly, this timeframe correlates to about the time most fetuses begin to move in the womb.

But aside from the evidence which leads to the preceding conclusions, there is another principle to consider: Namely, that it is the height of conceit to presume to dictate what other people can or cannot do with their own bodies – much less what is inside their bodies – which originated from inside their bodies in the first place!

Anti-abortionists are incredibly arrogant, at least in the case of early term pregnancies, for they negate the rights of those who already exist – which are the physical and spiritual parents – in favor of an organic machine that is likely not yet occupied. Put bluntly, by way of analogy, anti-abortionists demand we let the tail wag the dog.

People who demand control over the inside of other people's bodies remind me of slaveholders, those self-righteous demons of yesteryear who thought it fair to own other people and tell them when, and who, to breed with.

Blinded By Pride

He shouted that God is great and wished death to infidels. It was an angry response after someone had ridiculed Mohammed, and I couldn't help thinking that religious zealots remind me of rabid dogs when they threaten violence over an insult. When will they grow up? People who would commit murder over of an insult, real or imaginary, are a disgrace to humanity.

In the past, I was active in stopping Christian prayers that had been creeping into government meetings. My efforts included articles, letters, emails, phone calls, and numerous occasions where I spoke or gave presentations in front of Boards of Supervisors. Some of those meetings were full houses, jam packed with Christians and their priestcrafters, most of whom were hostile towards me, while the others quietly supported their hatred.

Yet, for all of the hateful looks and snide remarks, for all of the angry emails and nasty calls I received – not once was I physically attacked, or even threatened with such by Christians. Had I done those same things regarding Islam in a predominately Muslim country, not only would I have been beaten and jailed repeatedly, I would have been killed on some occasions.

So between Christian and Islamic influenced cultures, there is a tangible difference in the degree of mental illness they represent (only we know the true God and you must agree with us). That having been said, much of the betterment is due to western laws guaranteeing freedom of religion and separation of church and state.

In closing, Islam deserves derision, which should continue non-stop until the violent mutts within that religion are cast out by its other followers. So with that in mind, and knowing that any religion is a terminal illness when it's held in higher esteem than loving each other, perhaps the next time someone tells me they're a proud Muslim I will offer my condolences.

Lottery Elections & Voting Reform

A one party political system is a dictatorship. A two party political system is the same tyranny if one group controls both. And this is the situation the United States is dangerously approaching, because corporate billionaires now choose the candidates in every national election. In other words, no politician can afford to run for the higher offices without the support of the wealthy, so candidates promote policies that favor the tiny minority of rich people – at the expense of the vast majority of regular citizens.

A fair political arena would not only allow, but encourage, a multitude of opinions, instead of just two versions of the same monopoly. Indeed, a proper election system would have numerous candidates, all running as independents, without parties. In this way, politicians would stand or fall on their own merits, rather than because of their promoters.

One solution for getting independent candidates into government again is to have all elections begin with lotteries. In addition, all losing votes should rollover to another candidate until just one remains with the most ballots cast in their favor.

Though slight variations might be needed for some individual states, the method of Lottery Elections is simple and uses a general format as follows...

President and Vice-President

- Recent Governors or Congresspersons may register for the lottery.
- Randomly chosen candidates selected from this pool run for election.
- Public television carries candidate debates/discussions.
- Most votes wins President and second most Vice-President.

State Office (Governors or Congresspersons)

- Current or recent District Representatives may register for the lottery.
- Randomly chosen candidates selected from this pool run for election.
- Public television carries candidate debates/discussions.

<u>District Representatives/Regional Offices</u>

• Current or recent Local Representatives may register for the lottery.
• Randomly chosen candidates selected from this pool run for election.
• Public television carries candidate debates/discussions.

<u>Local Representative (City/County Councils)</u>

• Local residents may register for the lottery.
• Randomly chosen candidates selected from this pool run for election.
• Public television carries candidate debates/discussions.

Additional rules include that officials may only serve one elected term at each level of government service. Nor may they be paid lobbyists after leaving office. And again, every vote cast for a losing candidate rolls over until the most popular candidate is determined and declared the winner.

The way "rollover" works is that voters rate every candidate in preferential order when they vote. For example, if five candidates are running for President, you vote for one, but also select your 2nd preference, 3rd preference, etc. This eliminates less wanted candidates from winning by a fluke. History shows that contestants are occasionally so similar that they split the vote and a much less wanted candidate wins. Rollover prevents this. Here is an example to clarify the concept further:

Candidate A: Different than other candidates. Gets 4% of the votes.
Candidate B: Different than other candidates. Gets 6% of the votes.
Candidate C: Nearly identical to candidate D. Gets 28% of the votes.
Candidate D: Nearly identical to candidate C. Gets 30% of the votes.
Candidate E: Different than other candidates. Gets 32% of the votes.

Without rollover, Candidate E wins narrowly. But with rollover, losing votes go to the next selection a voter made. In this example, Candidate C or D would be the second choice for almost everyone that voted for either of them. So Candidate D would win by a huge margin when most of C's votes rolled over to D as their second choice. (Note the low vote count is always redistributed first.) In this example, even if every voter for A had selected B for their second choice, B would still only have 10%. So now B is also eliminated and both A and B have their votes redistributed to the next choice on their ballots (who is not yet eliminated). This goes on until the winner is determined.

Security is another important consideration...

Computer vote counting risks the theft of entire elections by a very small group of people. In addition, it is too easy to invade privacy if who you voted for is tracked electronically.

Manual counting deters theft, yet ensures voter privacy. The volunteers who donate time to count votes during election years have always enjoyed this community service anyway, and with everyone watching each other count, plus all the double checking, the overall results are almost impossible to steal. Given the massive benefits, it doesn't hurt to wait a few hours for election results to come in.

As an extra safeguard, ballots would be paper and designed similar to raffle tickets. This means every voter is given a double ballot with a unique serial number printed on both halves. The voter retains the duplicate stub after punching both halves in a voting booth. Voters can then go online and anonymously reference their ballot's serial number against a registry of votes cast. Any discrepancies would be addressed by visiting the local voting commission, stub in hand, to correct the error.

Lottery elections mean the end of career politicians. Plus, they ensure the better candidates can rise to the top by requiring elections after the drawings. They would result in the restoration of true citizen politicians and curtail the influence of the wealthy, whose total domination of election funding has effectively purchased the government for their own use.

Lastly, the structure guarantees that the most important offices have candidates with sufficient experience in government.

Brainwashed

We know that a person's mind influences their actions. So our behavior could be called the output of the mind, at least in general terms. This begs the question: What about mind input?

The past few decades have seen dozens of large U.S. media corporations merged into just six giant conglomerates. They own almost all of mainstream media, including film, television, radio, newspapers and magazines. Most of the internet has been captured, too, with government help, no less. The problem is that those company's major stockholders, typically billionaires, select the boards of directors, who in turn set the management that chooses what the public sees and hears – and how it's presented. Obviously, the slant is to benefit those wealthy owners.

Especially disconcerting is the pathetic state of the major news outlets, which have become nothing more than the public relations arm of the military-industrial complex. The same people own it all. And they aim to keep it that way.

Having conquered our information systems, the wealthy have also developed a stranglehold on Congressional policymaking. In fact, corrupted lawmakers voted that corporations should now be treated like people, a perverse near opposite of why corporations came to exist in the first place. Meanwhile, real humans are increasingly regarded as mere equipment and have less control of their government than any time since the American Revolution. This is largely because mass media is used by its rich owners to subtly promote agendas which decrease our civil rights and income, while they get corporate immunity and skyrocketing profits.

We have, however, maintained our conceited delusions of superiority over all other nations, which the propagandists peddle to our vanity in place of real knowledge and compassion. This is wickedly brilliant, since it's much cheaper for the wealthy than treating us fairly, which would then be followed by our demands that they treat the rest of the world better, too.

One proof of this homeland brainwashing is that among the major Western nations, we are the only one that has not implemented

Medicare/Universal Healthcare for all its citizens. Yet our medical expenses are twice as much as those other countries and our life spans are shorter. Other nations are awakening to see themselves as a family, but here, we primitively cling to competition as more important than cooperation. It's out of balance.

We may think we're superior, but most of the world sees the United States as selfish, stupid and violent. This is not 1945 – and the criticism is valid.

No longer the moral icon among the nations of the world, we are morphing into a military and police state with an economy that is dependent on war. Almost the only thing our nation excels at is the creation of soldiers, spy technologies, and the export of weapons, mercenaries, and military advisors.

Adding to this sad state of affairs, the owners of our military-industrial complex have manipulated government policies to decrease funding and lower expectations in our public schools, which is no concern to the rich, since their children attend private schools. Decades ago, the wealthy foresaw the economic parity that was coming for the nations of the world. Their only choice was to either share the blessings of life more equitably, or find ways to dumb down and cower the masses so they could maintain their lavish lifestyles.

Once world famous, our public schools are being reduced to daycare centers and half of all teachers quit within five years. Most high school students graduate with minimal skills and precious little cognitive ability. These youngsters are woefully unqualified for the modern workplace and soon discover that their only employment choices in the United States workforce are as soldiers or policemen, that is, if they want to earn enough money to support a family. College is not a viable option for many of them, either financially or academically, so those who remain outside this new national order are destined for poverty, working a lifetime at minimum wage.

Adding to the problem is the entertainment industry, which specializes in movies and video games that teach us to revel in military and police work, or related careers. These fields are expanding because the plutocracy needs them in order to keep control abroad – and control at home. Just watch television any night of the week and you can plainly see their social engineering in the programming. Almost every show involves murders or police related work, usually both. By age 18 the average child in the United States has seen over 100,000 simulated killings. But what they hardly ever see is the multitude of real fatalities we cause, because the information about these crimes is suppressed from public view, lest the wealthy suffer the economic and legal backlash that broad public awareness would cause.

Once our leaders taught us that adults should stand up for what is right. Now they imply that grown-ups don't question authority and do what they're told. No thank you. Real adults obey the golden rule.

But if you watch mainstream news, everything is rosy as airhead spokesmodels ignore our nation's madness in exchange for suckling money from the crotch of billionaires... What endless wars? No dead soldiers are ever seen. No dead civilians are ever seen. No broken hearted survivors are ever shown wailing in grief. And always, always, always, we are in the right. To hear our newscasters tell it, any nation broken by our selfishness deserves their river of tears. And if you fight against that wickedness, then you risk corrupt officials drowning you in your own.

Another example of the brainwashing is how the owners of major media outlets prevent serious, in-depth discussions about how badly the world's resources are being strained. And as they gloss over the problem, the other corporations they own are raping the environment unchecked by even basic common sense. Consider the contrast: It took 200,000,000 years for oil, gas and coal to be formed – that we will consume in 200 years. The same astronomical period of time was required for the mountains to rise, but now we blast an entire peak into gravel in a single second. These things will not grow back.

The profound dichotomy that is splitting western society needs to be examined. Why does the percentage of our citizens in poverty keep rising? Unable to support their families, they skimp on essentials, have no health care, and increasingly find themselves among the homeless. Yet this is happening while the income of the wealthiest is rising faster than any time in history! Something is very wrong. Only a child – or a demon – believes a person is entitled to make 200,000 times more per year than some of their full-time employees – who still need food stamps to survive. But that is what some executives are making compared to minimum wage employees.

Three fallacies mass media, government agencies, and corrupt politicians keep selling us are: The wisdom of trickle-down economics. The wealthy are job creators. Our leadership protects the masses. All are patently false.

In the case of trickle-down economics, we only need to consider the history of mankind, which shows that the powerful have always taken more than their fair share from the commoners. Unlike a family, wherein the strong uplift the weak, the hierarchy of trickle-down economics is akin to royalty controlling feudal lords, who in turn control the peasants… And it yields the same impoverished results.

As for the wealthy being job-creators, that is equally absurd. From Henry Ford to the Wright Brothers, Microsoft to Google, history shows it is small businesses that invent the new industries that create new wealth. When these companies mature, having spawned numerous competitors, then they only vie with each other for market share. If one corporate behemoth adds 5,000 jobs, then another one loses 5,000.

Lastly, the rich have never protected us. This fiction only serves to distract us from the truth that our nation is an abuser, both at home and abroad, and that we have been victimizing parts the world for a long time now. Yet the billionaire controlled mouthpieces of nightly news keep leading us to kill foreigners so the plutocracy can control the world's natural resources.

Of course, as I mentioned earlier, it's hard to see this in most media coverage because they no longer show the tears of our vanquished. Honest reporting ruined Vietnam's corporate cash cow by showing the war's horrors, which in turn reversed public opinion that once supported our involvement. Truthful news is very bad for the bottom line when your business is taking advantage of others, and the aristocracy doesn't intend to let it happen again. This is why they pander to our vanity and conceit, always subtly assuring us that other cultures are inferior. That is the unspoken lie that is always implied about the people we kill, though it is only about the money for our masters. Just as they led us to ravage the American Indian for free land, enslave the Africans for cheap labor, then slaughter the Vietnamese and Central Americans to install profit based political systems, so it is we now crush Middle Easterners to muscle in on their oil wealth.

Stop and think. If someone doesn't like us, how is that permission to kill them? Yet a single Saudi Arabian, living in Pakistan, was used to popularize the military conquest of Iraq and Afghanistan, neither of which had injured us in the slightest. Nor were they planning to. We initiated those wars to destabilize their countries so we could increase our influence over their natural resources and politics. In other words, it was mostly about the money we could make, while a million of them died, two million were injured, and three million were made refugees. And this is only part of the story, since secret intelligence operations have been undermining the entire region for decades. Yet none of this is featured on the evening news, more accurately described in today's world as the all-day propaganda. Once we led by example, but now we lead by the sword and call it wisdom.

Here is the painful truth about our beloved United States: Over and over, our political leaders have led us astray after selling us out for money and power. And the entire spectrum of major media, now representing the wealthy first and foremost, has become the plutocracy's biggest asset in brainwashing us to do their evil deeds. Because of that, among the so-called modern nations, we have become the bloodiest government in the world – and one of the most selfish to its own people.

I return to my original question: What about mind input? You wouldn't eat dirt and you shouldn't allow it mentally.

Getting your news from independent sources is mandatory if you really want to be informed. This means going to the internet or small print publications; but even here, caution is required, as more outlets are being established, purchased, or influenced by the rich. All major websites will soon be controlled and free speech is dying.

The Dark Ages of scientific and philosophical ignorance came to an end with The Reformation, which forced the separation of church and state.

The most important thing for our world right now is the separation of business and state. Perhaps another Age of Enlightenment would follow.

Crime of the Century

There are thousands of steel framed skyscrapers throughout the world. Not once have any of them suddenly collapsed without the use of explosives, until September 11, 2001 – according to our government.

And on that amazing first time in history, not just one, but three of them crumbled!

In addition, if that is not astonishing enough, all three went down as straight as arrows. In other words, they literally collapsed into their own footprints! Moreover, and this almost miraculous, all three buildings fell close to, or at, the speed of gravity! But honest structural engineers will tell you those things are impossible due to the massive steel beams woven throughout them during construction...

What really happened?

The so-called investigation by our government says it was the result of fires, but the blazes were all quite small. On the other hand, explosives fit the evidence perfectly. Every floor, in every building, shattered one after the other, with precision robotic timing, and then fell with perfect symmetry. There was no jagged breakage between the floors or on any of the sides as they crumbled. You can see it in the video recordings, especially with building 7. In the construction business they call such a thing controlled demolition, which is exactly what happened that day to all three buildings.

The official story behind the events is impossible. Consider some of the many things that should make you question the government's explanation of what happened at the World Trade Center...

Beforehand

• The skyscrapers were built to withstand airplane crashes.
• The skyscrapers were built to withstand raging infernos.
• New shell companies became WTC tenants in preceding months.
• Abnormal increase of new faces working night shifts.
• Months of private maintenance work in elevator shafts.
• Several complete facility "power downs" in the preceding weeks.
• Osama Bin Laden was a former CIA operative.

- Bush and Bin Laden families have been acquaintances for decades.
- Bush's father, also a President, was former head of the CIA.
- Bush's brother and cousin were officers of WTC security company.
- PNAC wanted "New Pearl Harbor" to motivate public for war.

At That Time

- Air traffic controller alerts were stalled by officials.
- NORAD was told to stand down when planes deviated off course.
- Bush socialized 25 minutes after being told a 2nd plane hit.
- Cheney was in White House command center during the event.
- Nano-thermite (high-tech explosive) residue was everywhere.
- Witnesses heard explosions on all the floors, even basements.
- Fires in all 3 buildings miniscule compared to construction standards.
- Jet fuel and office fires burn 1,000 degrees cooler than molten steel.
- Hot steel doesn't shatter, it bends.
- Some alleged hijackers reportedly seen right after (not seen since).
- Insurance company for WTC buildings paid billions on new policies.
- Airline stocks were ten to one in favor of "put" versus "call" orders.
- Planes made maneuvers that novice pilots could not perform.
- WTC building 7 housed clandestine CIA offices.

Afterwards

- No evidence of attack by any Muslim country.
- The "terrorists" were Saudis but Iraq was immediately blamed.
- Airplane black boxes failed or were not recovered – all 8 of them.
- Government has classified over 3,000 files.
- Government falsified results in its sham investigation.
- Bin Laden's family members flown out of U.S. 9/12 w/o questioning.
- President and Vice President refused to testify under oath.
- President and Vice President refused to testify separately.
- President and Vice President refused to testify publically.
- President and Vice President's testimony is sealed.
- Debris shipped to Asian scrap companies before investigation.
- Molten steel in lower levels, 80 stories below fires and 2 weeks after.
- Millions in airline stock trade profits uncollected (fear of inquiry).
- Kuwaiti gold supposedly missing from vaults under WTC 1 and 2.
- Key people surrounding the events have died suspiciously.
- Wikipedia write-ups are repeatedly ghost edited to be neutered.

• Mainstream media portrays those who ask questions as unstable.
• Mainstream media suppresses info and free speech about the events.

The problem so many citizens have in accepting what really happened is that they cannot imagine any of their leaders being that wicked, because they would never do such things themselves. But do people become billionaires making 200,000 times more per year than some of their employees because they care about others? And these icons of selfishness are the ones who install our leaders, who in turn approve the heads of our various "defense" organizations. These two groups are required to do their master's bidding or they can never advance their careers. Maintaining and expanding our corporate empire is our military's primary function. Major General Smedley Butler, in his day the most decorated Marine in history, was right about our wicked leaders and corporate overlords, and that was almost a century ago!

Consider the results of 9/11...

• The United States increased its influence on OPEC policies.
• The United States increased its influence on Middle East politics.
• The United States and Israel increasingly alter Middle East culture.
• Radical Zionism has increased its power in Israel.
• CIA conducting covert operations in dozens of Islamic countries.
• Habeas Corpus and parts of our Bill of Rights revoked by Patriot Act.
• Constitution itself essentially revoked by Patriot Act.
• Citizen tracking from cradle to grave, including all computer activity.
• Government can give prison sentences without trials or hearings.
• Government can assassinate citizens without trials or hearings.
• Torture and rendering legalized.
• Police state laws are proliferating.

Most wealthy people are delighted to see these changes, since they view common folks as disposable commodities, necessary only as equipment. Like the royalty of days gone by, these kind of people are expert at taking advantage of others – using brute force if they can get away with it, and when they can't, their every kindness is weighed against the probability of an excess return. And sadly, for the first time since the Reformation, they are reversing the gains of the common man in the western nations. The kings and queens of yesterday have been replaced by billionaires, whose dynasties also go on for generations.

There are dozens of other points and unanswered questions, as well, but I skipped them in the interest of brevity, as this article was not intended to be an exhaustive discussion. This is just a quick list of things to consider for those who are unfamiliar with the topic.

We will probably never know the truth behind the scenes in this lifetime, though I'm sure a higher power will sort out the cosmic arithmetic eventually, in this age or the next. But one thing is certain: We have not been told the truth by our government! The crime of the century was our own doing, at least in part. Perhaps our top intelligence officials even authored the plan from start to finish. But at a minimum, 9/11 was facilitated and then covered up by the secret services that make our country the world's de facto ruler. It is not without reason that we have over 1,000 military bases, installations, and information gathering offices in every corner of the globe, or that we spend approximately 50% of our nation's annual budget on things directly or indirectly related to the military. Would you spend half your money on something and never use it?

How could it happen?

International war conspiracies require involvement of the highest levels of government and clandestine military branches. They were the specific authors of 9/11. They know how to find ways to please their wealthy masters. In other words, they are not the root of the problem. That distinction goes to the super-rich, most of whom have little or no conscience. And they have no fear of prison for the things they influence, since they are never directly involved. Their minions either do the things that help billionaires keep taking more than their fair share, or strings get pulled, careers are suddenly ended, and new faces take the stage as spokesmodels for the status quo.

Mainstream media outlets, which the wealthy also own, imply that people who question official government explanations are crazy. This intimidates most critics from speaking up and keeps the bulk of the sheeple from actually thinking. But intelligent people know those news outlets are nothing more than the public relations departments of those corporations and their moguls.

These new age monarchs control armies of sycophants, who sell-out their integrity to ensure their benefactor's continued supremacy as the masses toil away their lives for the barest minimums. The reality is that the super-rich have conquered democracy with corruption and mutant capitalism. One look at our Congress is all the evidence needed, for our high officials are dependent on multi-millionaire and billionaire sponsors for the cost of their elections, basically purchasing their esteemed positions. The result is that democratic leaders have become mere employees of the world's financial elite, while the military enforces their monopolistic designs. It's always about the money and power.

The United States has a long history of falsifying information or provoking other nations in order to justify going to war, (for example, the Gulf of Tonkin incident, which we manufactured in order to justify entering the Vietnam War). In that same vein, our government has wanted a greater say in the business and politics of the Middle East for a long time – and now we have it. This is thanks to manipulating the public to support the overthrow of nations, achieved by blaming 9/11 on "terrorists" and then transferring the guilt to an entire region and religion.

On a side note, for the first time in history, zealots of the Christian and Jewish religions are in complete agreement, having been herded by wicked shepherds to support attacking any Islamic country. But they are both just as sick as Islam, as all three of them shamefully pretend to speak for god. (Everyone has access to the spirit of God, much better described as the spirit of love and reason, which communicates with all of us at the highest level each of us is able to understand. No intermediaries are necessary.)

Again, I know that many citizens have great difficulty believing our highest government officials and military leaders could have had a hand in something so evil, but we've been doing such things for over a century, and the evidence of our complicity on 9/11 is overwhelming. The only question is to what degree our involvement extends.

Why Socialism Wins

The first principle of reason is to treat others as you would be treated. The concept is innate knowledge and even infants understand it, though they lack the ability to articulate the concept. Indeed, by the time a child can talk, this idea is the first wisdom that they can express with words. In fact, so exceptional is this one single principle, it is literally the only thing that all rational adults agree on.

Certainly many people do not obey this "golden rule," especially among the young, for we all cling to selfishness, but no one denies it. To do so would publicly humiliate oneself, since the idea carries its own authority.

Reasoning also concludes there is another facet to this universal principle, which is that we should love each other. This is also self-evident, for no rational person wishes others to be unkind to them.

More than anywhere else in our lives, love and reason are seen in their fullest flower within the family unit. Our spouses, children, parents, friends, and relatives are the happiest part of our lives. So the concept as it applies to society is clear: Love and the golden rule must be the core foundation in any proper system of governance – and the most loving and reasonable structure is a family.

What are the basic rights of every family member? Food, shelter, clothes, and to be cared for when one is unable to provide for themselves. In other words, one's basic rights are one's basic needs. Therefore, these are the basic rights of every citizen. This is altogether fair, since every one of us lives under a government that we did not design, but are subjected to, just as we were born into a family over which we had no control. And taking the principle further, anything that controls others must be benevolent in its design and behavior, or it forfeits the right to lead, just as bad parents lose custody of their children.

The family principle always applies, whether at the top where the system is designed, or at the bottom in prisons, where citizens are sent to reconsider their violations of the golden rule and spare the innocent further suffering, just as wayward children are sometimes punished by being confined to their room.

The government must reflect that we are all one family – the most loving societal structure we know – or the system is wrong.

And therein is a fundamental problem with raw capitalism. When a system allows domination so severe it guarantees some citizens are homeless, then the family structure becomes like a master controlling slaves, or like heartless royalty having little concern for sacrificed peasants. In fact, capitalism with no checks and balances is essentially a form of war, since it not only rewards taking advantage of others, it encourages it. Insult to injury, it even reduces charity, for any generous act is a possible step towards one's own poverty without the safety net of minimum standards. "Everyone for themselves" fails miserably without the basics guaranteed as a counterbalance for everyone.

On the other hand, communism, with its fictional equality of every member, also falls short. Though everyone may be equal in value, not everyone is equal in abilities. A dandelion is not the same as a sequoia. Moreover, if everybody receives an equal share of the fruits of labor, no matter what effort they contribute, then laziness flourishes and creativity dies. In short, the system collapses under the weight of freeloaders, while the lack of tangible reward for extra effort is demoralizing. "One size fits all" fails miserably without a counterbalance for individuality.

So again, socialist nations that guarantee the basic necessities of life to their citizens have seen it results in a greater sense of being a family. Their people know they are part of the same team, unlike it is in raw capitalism, and they haven't sacrificed their individual rights and rewards which happens with communism.

The family principle also makes it easy to see how citizens should pay for government. Obviously, the higher the income an individual has, then the higher percentage of taxes they must pay for the upkeep of the family. Those who earn very little should pay the lowest percentage. Parents always spend a much greater percentage of their money on the children, rather than the other way around.

What about maximums or minimums on how much income a citizen can earn?

First, the idea of a maximum is contrary to the idea of life itself. Limits to an individual's growth should be subject only to fairness and the needs of fellow citizen family members. While peers must not suffer hardship because of another's prosperity, restricting someone's growth out of envy or laziness is profoundly wrong. So there should not be income caps. But if some individuals are earning, for example, billions of dollars per year, then obviously they should be paying a much, much higher percentage in income tax, which is the way our government once was. After all, everyone earns their living with the direct and indirect help of countless other people, yet it is a fact that many of our richest citizens are paying the lowest percentage in taxes. And that is criminal.

As for minimums, even though babies burden the upkeep of the home, (meaning criminals and those who refuse to pull their weight), they are still granted the basic necessities of life. If one is unsure exactly what those minimums should be, then the place to start is by guaranteeing that law-abiding citizens are entitled to at least whatever is granted to prison inmates.

'But everyone will freeload' say our greedy masters. Nonsense. Think it through… Rooming in jail-sized spaces, little privacy, public showers and toilets, rules and curfews, and doing community service work for your upkeep. The concept is more of a halfway house – a bridge. The point is, family members would not be cast out. By way of analogy, who among us would willingly allow their selfish teenagers to perish, even if they were lazy and self-indulgent?

Also, never forget that some people in dire circumstances are innocent, perhaps even sainted. We've all seen people who were injured or infirmed by accident or by the hand of others, while some precious individuals are suffering because they voluntarily interceded to help someone else!

Yet, while this goes on, some wealthy people are making 200,000 times more per year than minimum wage. How can anyone with great wealth ignore the poverty of their employees? Only super-rich sociopaths and their sycophants even try to justify it, though every wealthy person attained their lofty position with an incalculable amount of help from the rest of humanity. These are peers we are talking about, equal human beings! Who can justify the obscenity of so many people unable to support themselves, much less their families? And none of this begins to the address the multitude of citizens that are unemployed or underemployed.

But all people will never be wise, for there will always be children, so to speak, meaning selfishness and crimes will continue, and sometimes succeed, to the detriment of many innocent people. And though punishment will come to pass for the unloving, in this age or the next, the remedy for victims is often beyond our mortal power to resolve. Nevertheless, we need to do what we can.

So what choices do we have?

Should we leave it to "god" to provide assistance to our brethren? Or is that just a miserable excuse we use to justify doing nothing?

Or should we emulate the highest principle in every day and age, which is love and the golden rule, and become the family we were meant to be.

Palestine... The Unholy Land

For almost 80 years, the Palestinians and Jews have been fighting with each other. It's the latest installment of arguments that began 4,000 years ago.

Did God give the land of Palestine to certain people, or not?

If God did not, then who put lies in God's mouth in order to steal?

And if God did, then what was promised?

These questions have never been answered to the satisfaction of everyone involved, and the dialogue between the parties always turns into violence.

With that in mind, the key to solving the problem in Palestine is to consider the illnesses of most of the people involved, who claim to understand God better than everyone else and think they are God's favorite. By illnesses, I specifically mean the religions that most of the people involved are following, which are Judaism and Islam, and also Christianity, which has generally supported the Jews recently. Since all three groups have elevated written words to be the voice of God, instead of trusting the innate authority of love and the golden rule, it may be possible to use information from those ancient texts to fix the problem.

Therefore, the following remedy for the situation in Palestine will be based on scripture and common sense. This is regardless of what may be the actual historical truth, long since lost in time, if it was ever known by them in the first place. In the interest of comprehension for the layman, this account will be as simple and abbreviated as possible.

We begin with Abraham. He is a physical and/or spiritual patriarch to the people of all three mental illnesses previously mentioned. Abraham had two sons, Ishmael and Isaac. The Palestinians trace their lineage from Ishmael, son of Abraham. The Jews trace their lineage from Judah, son of Jacob, son of Isaac, son of Abraham.

God made promises to Abraham that he would bless him by making nations of his offspring, and also that all nations of the world would be blessed through him. Many years later, God made similar promises to

Abraham's grandson, Jacob, whom he renamed Israel. These promises were both physical and spiritual in nature.

Were the promises fulfilled?

Israel was already a great nation under David, and then Solomon. As for the promises that were spiritual in nature, a vast multitude say these were fulfilled by Jesus. He was a Jewish man who taught that the real kingdom of God is spiritual in design, rather than physical, because love and the golden rule are the key to life and the highest authority.

But however you view the promises made to Abraham, whether you see them as past, present, or future – or as fiction that was written by priestcrafters to obtain power and revenue – the critical point is this: The Jews do not represent all of Israel, but only Judah, one of his many sons.

Here is more background on this...

Israel's descendants would eventually refer to themselves as being from a certain "tribe," meaning which of his 12 sons was their earliest ancestor. But before that came to pass, Israel (Jacob), his sons, and their families, went to Egypt where one son was already located. Generations later, his many descendants then migrated to the Sinai Desert under the leadership of Moses. Here the tribes cast lots to divide the land they were about to invade, called Canaan (today's Palestine) and the descendants of Judah (Judeans/Jews) were given the southernmost portion of Palestine,

The tribes then lived in peaceful alliance with each other and Israel eventually became a powerful nation under King David, then a world crossroads under his son, King Solomon (both Judeans).

But there was great unrest over the high taxes imposed by Solomon to support his extravagant lifestyle. When he died, the other tribes petitioned the new king, Rehoboam (son of Solomon), to reduce taxes. Instead of addressing their legitimate complaints, the childish new king insulted them, which caused the other tribes to expel Judah from the nation of Israel.

Thus, Israel and Judea became separate countries (sometimes called the northern and southern kingdoms by Bible scholars). It was this way for centuries, with the two even warring against each other on occasion.

244

And then the physical nation of Israel ended.

The kingdom of Assyria rose to power and conquered Israel. They took everything of value back to their homeland, including educated citizens and tradesmen, leaving only the poorest peasants behind, who remained subjected to foreigners. The land ceased to be called Israel and eventually became known as Samaria, the name of its capitol and most influential city.

After this, the Babylonian empire came to power and conquered Judea. And they did the same thing to the Judeans that the Assyrians had done to the Israelites. However, when Persia conquered Babylon several decades later, some of the Jews who had not assimilated returned to Jerusalem, rebuilt their temple, and gradually wrote the first versions of most of the Old Testament books.

Meanwhile, centuries passed. The Israelites (all the other tribes of the northern kingdom) never returned, but instead were absorbed into other nations. Eventually the Greeks invaded Judea, then the Romans, and others followed after that. All of the once independent nations in the land of Palestine were continually subjected to one foreign power after another.

In every era, Samaria, the majority of ancient Israel, was considered ethnically distinct from Judea. It was this way even when Rome managed all of Palestine (including Galilee, formerly northern Samaria), as one province. In fact, Judea had been a separate country for close to 1,000 years by the time of Roman rule, and the nation of Israel had not existed for many centuries.

Understand, it wasn't only foreign rulers that considered the Judeans a separate people, because the Jews themselves thought so, routinely insulting their northern neighbors by calling them "half-breeds." This disparaging attitude is especially telling, given that many Jews lived among the Samaritans and Galileans, many of whom shared the blood of their brother tribes lost to antiquity.

Because of constant rebellions by the Jews against their Roman occupiers, particularly in Jerusalem, the Romans and Jews fought two wars, both crushing defeats for Judea. The first was just a few decades after Jesus died and the second was about 100 years later. After the second war, Rome was fed up with the endless insurrections and declared that every Jew must leave the land of Palestine, or die. So this edict not only applied to Judea, but also Samaria and Galilee, and thus the Jewish diaspora was completed. From this point on there were almost no Jews in Palestine for about 1,800 years.

In the last 140 years, and especially in the last 80 years, descendants of Judah moving to the land of Palestine have gone from owning about 1% of the land to possessing nearly 80% of it. Nearly all of the increase has been forcibly taken from the Palestinians and other people living in the old northern kingdom. But most of this occupied land does not belong to the Jews – according to their own record, for the nation of Israel (all the other tribes) has been gone over 2,500 years. All the returning ancestors of Judah are entitled to – assuming they are entitled – is that which was called Judea, their old southern kingdom.

Also, their new nation should have been named Judea again. This logic was ignored by the returning Jews, who named their new country Israel, the same name as the long extinct great nation which once included all 12 tribes and far more territory. But the one remaining tribe, Judah, should not be allowed to claim false borders in order to annex all of ancient Israel, which God never gave them, and which they have never ruled. Stated plainly, the old northern kingdom does not belong to the Jews.

Not only is this is this logical based on scriptures, it fits historically. Those areas were occupied by the ancestors of Palestinians and other nations before, during, and after Jesus' time, including 1,800 years after the diaspora with virtually no Judeans living there. It is only recently that the Jews have returned – or invaded – depending on one's point of view.

So let the Jews have the land of Judea, which is their original gift from God and includes Jerusalem. In return, the Palestinians keep Gaza and all of the old northern kingdom, including Tel Aviv, where ancestors of theirs and other nations have lived continuously for over 2,500 years.

After the land of Palestine becomes separate nations again, if the Jews want to expel any non-Jew from Judea because it pleases their sick Jewish God, then so be it. And if the Palestinians want to expel any non-

Muslim from their country because it pleases their sick Islamic God, then so be it.

It is a tragedy that Jews and Muslims have not elevated love and reason above all other things. The same could be said about Christians, who turned the great reformer Jesus into a new god business, ironically, after he rebuked the one built on Moses. Jesus called us brothers and sisters and taught that love and the golden rule should be our master. But instead of taking this great universal and eternal truth to heart, priestcrafters put him above us, so they can try to be above us in his absence. This is the same reason the other sicknesses put their icons Moses and Mohammed above us.

Religions are the spiritual equivalent of contagious physical illnesses. And anyone who puts anything above love and the golden rule is terminally ill.

Correspondence

Letter to Debbie

Hi Debbie:

With all due respect, and understanding that your passion for "love one another" is indeed the key to life, here are quite a number of miscellaneous thoughts you might want to consider...

Love is the only real authority that ever has, does, or will exist.

True religion is a personal matter and nothing about it, except love, is universal to us all.

Religions abound, their opinions presented like facts by charlatans who dare tell us they speak for God, as if they have some access to the Almighty that the rest of us do not.

If an individual begins thinking that he is better than other people then the spirit is displeased. So how does being a group of individuals (religion) improve the same mistake?

Love is the eternal life sustaining force in the spiritual realm, just as air is the life sustaining force in our physical realm.

A seed becomes a fetus in the womb. Then it is born an infant into a new world, but the placenta it was attached to and received nourishment from is discarded. Then that child one day becomes a parent itself, then grandparent... Likewise, love is the spiritual seed that begets goodness to grow within us, here in the womb of this earthly life. When we die here, it is simply our spiritual birth as a new child into a new world, while our body here is discarded, just as our placenta once was.

Churches and scriptures are all man-made, so even if they avoid the crime of telling us how and what to think, they are still other people suggesting those things. What we are, by definition, must outgrow such tutoring and find us thinking for ourselves. Not only would such a proxy be bad for spiritual adults, it is not even permitted, for to presume authority to think for a peer is as wicked as any conceit ever known.

A person may speak to the spirit of god, and a person may speak about god, but no person may speak for god.

251

We are all "christs" because we have all suffered unjustly at the hand of others.

If god is love, and love and money together is prostitution, then what is religion but spiritual harlotry perfected into a science.

Religions are the worst diseases in human history and are in fact the spiritual equivalent of a contagious illness. And putting the precepts of any religion above "love one another" is the spiritual equivalent of being terminally ill.

Compared to love, no religion has ever mattered, or ever will, except to the spiritually dead!

Christian mythology presents the Almighty as compelled to surrender the whole of creation to Satan, or come to earth and die. Has the pride of man become so great that nothing can flatter it except the suicide of his Creator?

When the church mythologists established their system they created and collected writings and managed them as they pleased. Centuries later they decided by voting which books of the collection they had made should be the word of God, and which should not. Those books which had a majority of votes are presented to us as God's official word.

Nothing that is said here applies with disrespect to the real character of Jesus Christ. The morality that he preached and practiced was of the most benevolent kind. Though similar systems of morality have been preached by many good men in all ages, it has never been exceeded by anyone. But the stories of Jesus, relating to the supernatural parts, have every mark of fraud and imposition stamped upon them.

No miracles are required to know that love is the key to eternal life. Jesus didn't invent love, he merely discovered its authority, like a multitude of others before and since.

The word prophet originally meant poet, and "prophesying" meant the art of making poetry to a tune upon a musical instrument. The Bible speaks of prophesying with pipes and horns, with harps and cymbals. If we now spoke of prophesying with a horn the expression would appear ridiculous. We are told of Saul being among the prophets, but we are not told what was prophesied because there was nothing to tell, for Saul prophesied badly, that is, he performed his part badly, for they say an "evil spirit from God came upon Saul." (An evil spirit from God?!)

We are told of the greater and the lesser prophets. They might as well tell us of the greater and the lesser God, for there cannot be degrees in prophesying. But there are degrees in poetry, and therefore the phrase is reconcilable to the case, when we understand it by the greater and the lesser poets.

On the topic of redemption: I think man stands the same with his Maker as he ever did.

Are we to have no word of God, no revelation? Yes! There is a Word of God; there is a revelation. The word of God is your conscience within you (the authority of love) and the creation we behold, and this is the word that no human invention can counterfeit or alter.

Man understands in the meaning of God "first cause," that is, the cause of all things. Incomprehensible as it is for a man to conceive what a first cause is, he believes it from the greater difficulty of disbelieving. It is indescribable to think that space can go on forever, but it is more difficult to conceive it ending. It is beyond the power of man to conceive eternity; but even harder to understand no time. In like manner of reasoning, everything we behold carries in itself the evidence that it did not make itself. Every man is evidence to himself that he did not create himself; neither could his father make himself, nor his grandfather, nor any of his race; neither could any tree, plant, or animal make itself; and it is the conviction arising from this evidence that carries us by necessity, to the belief of a first cause eternally existing. This is a nature totally different to any material existence we know of, and by this power all things exist; and man calls this "God."

It is a lie for the Christian system to call the sciences human inventions. It is only the application of sciences that is human. Man cannot make principles, he can only discover them. Every science has principles as fixed as those by which the universe is governed. Man can make or draw a triangle, therefore it may be said that a triangle is a human invention. But the triangle, when drawn, is just the image of the principle. The triangle does not make the principle, any more than a candle taken into a dark room made the chairs that before were invisible.

253

The advocates of the Christian system foresaw the knowledge that man would gain, so it became necessary to their purpose to reject the study of science. They even persecuted it and the age of scientific ignorance commenced with Christianity. It is nearly impossible to believe that any religion would call it wickedness to seek to discover the structure of the universe that God made, but the fact is too well established to be denied.

If we survey our world, we find every part of it crowded with life, from the largest animals to the smallest insects, and from there to others still smaller, totally invisible without a microscope. Every tree and plant, every leaf, serves not only as habitation, but as a world to some numerous life form. Since no part of our earth is left unoccupied, why suppose that the immensity of space is a naked void? There is room for millions of worlds as large as or larger than ours, each of them millions of miles apart from each other. In the midst of those reflections, what are we to think of the Christian system of faith?

There have been men who persuaded themselves that a pious fraud, under some circumstances, might be productive of good. But the fraud once established could not afterwards be explained, begetting the calamitous necessity of going on. The people who first preached the Christian system of faith, combining it with the morality preached by Jesus, persuaded themselves it was better than the heathen mythology that then prevailed. But from the first preachers the fraud went on to the second, and to the third, until the idea of its being a pious fraud became lost in the belief of its being true; and that belief was further encouraged by making a living by it. But though such belief, by such means, might become common among the laity, it is next to impossible to explain the continual persecution carried on by the church against the sciences and its professors; except the church knows it cannot hold its power without such oppression.

The Bible makes God act like an emotional man, that he would kill his son when he could not avenge himself any other way. But God is too good to do such a thing and too almighty to be under any necessity of doing so. Do you really think God told Abraham to kill his son? We put people in jail or asylums if they set out to do such a thing.

If I have already died in this body and am raised again in the same body, it is presumptive evidence that I shall die again. This kind of resurrection is a gloomy doctrine. Every animal in the creation exceeds our abilities at something. Winged creatures travel across land with greater ease than man while even the smallest fish swims better than us beyond comparison. Even the sluggish snail can ascend from the bottom of a pit. Caterpillars become butterflies and acorns become oaks, so the resurrection of the same body is far too little for all the powers and possibilities God has shown us.

Thought is of a different nature from everything we know and is essentially distinct from matter. Every time a specific thought takes place, in whomever, or whatever, that thought has the capacity of existing unaffected by whatever combination of matter it resides in. A thought therefore has, in itself, a capacity of being immortal, living wherever it is given a home, and living in as many homes as it is given. It stands to reason then, that a producer of thoughts can also be immortal. Therefore, our own self-consciousness of existence, which produces its own thoughts, can be immortal and exist independent from matter we formerly occupied.

If there ever was such a man as Adam, he was certainly a Deist. The only religion that has not been invented is pure and simple deism. But deism does not answer the purpose of despotic governments. They cannot lay hold of religion as an engine of power unless they mix it with human inventions and make their own authority a part. Neither does Deism answer the avarice of priests, who incorporate themselves and their sanctimonious functions with a religion and become, like the government, a party in the system. Deism teaches us all which is necessary to be known, without the possibility of being deceived by others. The creation is the work of God to the Deist, and his conscience subject to the authority of love is the word of God.

I am not worried about future existence. I am content with believing, even certain, that the power that gave me existence is able to continue it, with or without this body; and it appears to me more probable that I shall continue to exist hereafter than that I was brought into existence in the first place.

All religions believe in some kind of God. The things in which they disagree are the man-made additions annexed to that belief; and therefore, if ever a universal religion should prevail, it will not be by believing anything that is not already known to us all. The authority of love and the golden rule are known to us all, and they are the only things that all rational humans agree on. Therefore, love must be God.

Christians resort to what they call Scripture Evidence and Bible authority, to help them out. They confuse disputes about authenticity as disputes about doctrines. They use that multitude of man-made writings to prove any doctrine they want, but before the Bible can be admitted as proof, the Bible itself must be proved, for if the Bible is not true, it ceases to have authority and proves nothing. It has been the practice of Christian commentators and preachers to impose the Bible on the world as a mass of truth, the word of God. They have disputed and wrangled, and anathematized each other about the supposed meaning of parts and passages therein. One has insisted that such a passage meant one thing, another that it meant directly the contrary, and a third that it meant something different from both; and this they call understanding the Bible. The only thing they agree on is that everyone else knows less than themselves! They contend and wrangle, and in understanding the Bible, each understands it differently, but each understands it best. But instead of wasting their time in fractious disputes about doctrinal points drawn from the Bible, these men ought to know that the first thing to be understood is, whether there is sufficient proof for believing the Bible to be the word of God, or whether there is not? Plainly there is not.

It is said in the Bible that God spoke to Moses, but how do you know? Because, you say, the Bible says so. The Koran says that God spoke to Mohammed, do you believe that too? No. Why not? Because, you will say, you do not believe it. And so, because you do, and because you do not, is all the reason you can give for believing or disbelieving, except that you will say that Mohammed was an impostor. And how do you know Moses was not an imposter? All are impostors who pretend to hold verbal communication with the Deity.

The Bible represents God to be a changeable, emotional, vindictive Being; making a world, then drowning it, afterwards repenting, and promising not to do so again. He sets one nation to cut the throats of another, then stops the sun until the butchery is done. But the works of God in the Creation preach a different doctrine. In that vast volume, we see nothing to give us the idea of a changeable, emotional, vindictive

256

God. Everything we see there impresses us with a contrary idea – that of eternal order, harmony, and goodness as the sun and the seasons return at their appointed times.

That bloodthirsty man, called the prophet Samuel, makes God to say, (i Sam. xv. 3), "Now go and smite Amalek, and utterly destroy all that they have, and spare them not, but slay both man and woman, infant and suckling, ox and sheep, camel and ass." That Samuel or another impostor might say this, is what, at this distance of time, cannot be proved or disproved, but it is blasphemy to say that God decreed it. All our ideas of the justice and goodness of God revolt at such impious cruelty. It is not a God, just and good, but a devil, under the name of God, that the Bible describes! This slaughter was done by the express command of God? Lies! I will never believe any book that ascribes mass murders, cruelty and injustice to God and reject it as having any authority whatsoever.

Or consider a similar Bible decree, except this time God decreed that the virgin girls could be kept as spoils of war… Are we really to believe that orphans, now owned as sex slaves, by the murderers of their families, was the will of a God?

The businessmen who took control of Jesus' legacy were able to agree on one thing: If they put Jesus above us, then they could be above us in his absence. (The businessmen of Moses and Mohammed did the same thing with their icons.)

Almost the entirety of Jesus' original message was lost or altered. All but gone is the story of a demon who found the key to life (love one another) and tried to help us other demons find their way.

Love one another cannot be denied. The idea carries its own authority. And with this one giant pearl, a multitude of man-made fables annexed to it, for the purpose of power and revenue, is given the benefit of the doubt. But just like the Earth is no longer thought to be the center of the universe, so it is that speaking for God will pass away as the self-centered foolishness that it is.

Real religion is simply the practice of all of the fruits of the spirit of love with unity and goodwill towards all other life.

Letter to Allen

Hi Allen:

Thank you (and Patty) for entrusting me with the sale of your vacation home. It meant a lot that you bet on me, so to speak, and I was pleased to be successful, which in part was due to you.

More than that, how refreshing to meet a Christian who did not hurt my feelings for disagreeing (some) with their religious point of view.

As a gift, I hope you will accept the enclosed book, Selfish Young Man (parts 1 and 2), which I printed off my computer from the original manuscripts. Note that part 2 was never officially published like part 1.

Certain ideas carry their own authority. Examples would be love one another, do unto others as you would have done unto yourself, and everyone ruled by love has eternal life. Now combine those truths with the concept of intelligence as most men think of it, meaning I.Q. rather than L.Q. (love quotient). The former can be led astray without the latter in charge, but you already know this.

Let's suppose, only for the sake of discussion, that my understanding of Jesus is closer to correct than yours. What would that mean? Nothing. Calculators give a correct answer time after time. Computers are smart and getting smarter. Still, they are just machines and can never truly substitute for real interaction between independent life entities. IQ is nothing compared to LQ.

What all of this is leading to is another idea that carries its own authority: Whoever creates the most love in the world has done the best with their life.

Some years ago I watched a highly respected group of academics at a round table discussion. I was enjoying their scoffing at religions until one of them said of Christians "wait until they find out they pissed their lives away". How embarrassing – for him. Wait until he finds out that what you understand in life is meaningless compared to the love you create with your life. It's not what you know. It's what you do.

In closing, spiritually speaking, it will never matter if you or I believe things that turn out to be mistaken. What matters is the spirit of love, but you already know this, too.

Thank you again Allen. It was my pleasure to work with you and I wish you and yours all the best.

Interview with the Author

Q: Why did you self-publish?

A: I wanted to share what I've learned, to make a contribution to the public discourse. You won't hear most of what I have to say about religion from priestcrafters, though I'm sure a few independent scholars will appreciate my work. Nor will you hear opinions similar to mine on social issues from mainstream media, which long ago sold out to the wealthy. No traditional publisher would have considered printing something so critical of the status quo, plus, the work has little commercial value. They would have said it's too personal, too eclectic, or that I'm not a professional writer.

Q: Which books of the Bible are most important?

A: People are moved by different things and for different reasons, so there's no definitive answer. And time changes perspectives, too. As a child the Book of Proverbs was special to me. As I grew older the Book of Genesis became a favorite. Eventually, the Book of Job stood out most of all. It's the oldest work in the Bible, written even earlier than the Old Testament books, originating from outside of Jewish and Christian cultures. I like that Job expresses his true feelings and communicates directly with his god. No priestcrafters have beguiled his natural right and ability.

Q: Which translation of the Bible is best?

A: First, it's important to note that Bible study is not important for most people, nor are the words from any other religion. One's conscience, subject to the authority of love and the golden rule, is all anyone needs for true religion. In other words, there are an infinite number of personal religions that love and independent thinking creates in each of us individually, all of them superior to following someone else's god. Having said that, I think the best English version of the Bible was done by James Moffatt. It's hard to find a copy these days because priestcrafters fear the author's honesty and therefore pushed it out of favor. And his introduction at the beginning of that work is exceptional. He was also a very gifted linguist in both Latin and Greek, the two languages of the oldest versions of the books now called the Bible. Being able to correctly translate from the oldest scribed accounts in both languages was a big plus almost no other English speaking translator ever had.

Q: Do you think religions will survive in the future?

A: Yes. But as always, they will keep evolving. Our world is increasingly interconnected which leaves no choice but for religions to become more like philosophies in order to survive. And this is an improvement because it's getting harder to fool people by pretending to speak for god. The new problem is that science has become the most popular substitute for god. Like priestcraft, science is generally business minded, rather than a humanitarian endeavor. And science, by definition, means its conclusions are often found to be wrong at a later date. You cannot elevate anything above the only thing that stands forever, which is love and the golden rule, the two faces of the one eternal precept. Love is the action, the energy. The golden rule is the law, the framework.

Q: What do you think we take with us to the next life?

A: Not much, but there will be substantial improvement compared to what we started with in this life. I see us being able to hold on to the natural inclinations with die with. In other words, we keep the things that have become reflex to us. One of those things will be the love we feel for some other souls that were part of our lives here. We won't have to think about it. It just is. We will also have better ability to control our actions when an impulse is unloving. Thinking, though it has little power compared to reflex, is still a vast improvement over nothing when trying to avoid behaving badly.

Spiritually speaking, the physical example of childbirth is very revealing about our coming spiritual life, for a mother's feelings for a healthy newborn will soon eclipse the agony she just experienced. Similarly, our painful experiences as a human will fade away when we are born into the next life. From our first birth contraction, which is when we realize we are going to die someday, to the last contraction, which comes with actually dying, those memories will soon become too trivial to matter.

Q: Why did you stop writing about Christ and Christianity?

A: Years of studying yielded what I needed. The *Selfish Young Man* books were the result of decades of personal searching, written to the best of my ability and covering everything I felt moved to talk about. Even from the beginning I was including non-fiction poems and personal things in my writing, so it was natural to gravitate towards other topics, addressing them through poetry and articles. But after a very short time I felt I had done what I could with those things, too. With hindsight, I realize my solitary academic life was becoming unfulfilling and tiresome. Reading, writing, and especially reflection are certainly valuable, but there's a lot more to life.

Q: Do you envision marriage in the next life?

A: Yes, but not like it is in this life. I know that Jan and I will be friends forever, together whenever we both want to be. The way I see our future is perhaps best explained with an analogy... The stars are scattered everywhere, but all of them are usually in closer proximity to just one other sun. This is similar to how our feelings usually run deepest for just one person, or very few others, at any given time. So I think Jan and I, like the stars, will often be each other's closest neighbor as we grow through the ages. Our orbits will often take us closer to other stars, but our paths will always occasionally return us to being nearest each other for a time. Whenever that happens, I'm sure we'll relate the experiences we had while we were away from each other and share new adventures while we are together again. Jan once wrote to me, "My dreams will forever entwine with yours." I know she is right.

Q: How do you think we came to exist here?

A: I don't know, except that the power of love is part of the answer. But I do know why I am here. For me, this life is mostly a school where I am learning to love others. Looking at the two sides of love, giving and

263

receiving, it's clear that humans start this life almost exclusively receiving. Physical examples are too obvious to need mentioning. Spiritual examples are shown by our inherent self-centeredness at birth, which often expresses itself in ugly ways, especially in our youth. Thankfully, as we age we can develop more of a giving nature.

I have also come to believe we probably have always existed, or at least a part of us always has. The stars make a fine example to help explain this idea, too... They shine their light without reservation and planets gather round for gain. But eventually, the stars give and give until their light is exhausted and it's time to rest by sleeping. Continuing the analogy, their dying will not be forgotten by other stars, nor by grateful planets, now aspiring to be stars themselves, so all of them assist when possible to rekindle the essence of beings so loving that they died after giving their all. It makes sense that something that evolves into 100% give must eventually burn out, and therefore need to receive again. I am far from having that kind of love for others, but there's hope...

Once, when talking to my son about humanity, I remarked that comparing the difference between the light of man's goodness, versus that of higher life forms, would result in finding human brilliance to be pitch black by comparison. Without hesitation, he said something like: "Beings that powerful could see infrared, gamma and x-rays, so they would see our potential."

What a wonderful and encouraging observation!

Afterword

The biographical information in the introduction was included to help explain my obsessive search for answers to life's questions, and to show the effort I put into that quest. No doubt some readers will dislike my work, but no one can say I haven't studied.

The first *Selfish Young Man* is almost identical to this edition. Though my writing might be improved, especially as some parts are over 30 years old, I rejected the idea of updating the work. Substantive changes would be minimal, so it wasn't necessary.

Selfish Young Man Part II is nearly 15 years old. There are some places I edited for clarity.

The text in both of those books was reformatted, several headers were added, and some typos were corrected.

Generally, the articles and poems in *Wiser Old Man* were first written and published more than 10-12 years ago, but many of these pieces were re-published in various places, leading me to polish most of them over the years.

Any and all remaining Lake Publishing and author copyrights expire upon my passing and the entire work is thereafter public domain.

Thank you for letting me share my thoughts. I hope you found a few things that were worth your time.